Don't Read This Book!
It may cause a mid-life crisis!

Tom Tortorich

Kansas City, MO
www.GreenEffectMedia.com

Copyright © 2015 by Tom Tortorich

ISBN 978-0-9855535-5-5

Cover art by Scenes of Time photography.

www.ScenesofTime.com

This book is published in the spirit of Creative Commons by Green Effect Media, Kansas City, MO, as part of the copyleft movement.

Everyone is hereby encouraged to reproduce and distribute portions of this book, in whole or in part, without written permission of the publisher.

www.GreenEffectMedia.com

Printed in the United States of America.

First Edition: October 2015

*"Never give up on a dream
just because of the time
it will take to accomplish.
The time will pass anyway."*

—*Earl Nightingale*

Contents

Part One   1
Realizing the Life of your Dreams

Part Two   35
Transcending Cultural Conditioning

Part Three   81
Awakening to your Higher Self

Afterword   167
Personal Maxims of a Positive Enabler

Symbology on the Cover

*T*he cover is a photo I took on a trip to the Amazon Rainforest in Ecuador in 2011. As our canoe slowly glided out of the dense jungle that canopied the river, we emerged onto an ethereal lake just as the sun was setting.

Rain is constant in the rainforest, and a break in the storm clouds at sunset as we paddled out onto the lake yielded a view of a perfect rainbow, seen from end to end, and reflected in the perfectly still water beneath us.

I have never seen such a perfect reminder symbolizing the mutual interconnection of all things in this life. I have since learned that we can only see the reflection and connection of ourselves everywhere when our minds, like the water, are calm.

Symbols in nature like this have been appearing with much more frequency recently, as everyday I learn how to swim in the natural Flow of life more skillfully.

*That's what this book is about.
The photo is titled, "Circle of Life."*

T he Egyptian Ankh, standing in for the 'a' in the word 'crap' is also a reminder of interconnectedness, after a fashion,

It symbolizes aligning with the Higher Self, and also that our energies are best used when they are allowed to re-circulate back into ourselves, another, and everywhere.

When applied skillfully, our energies are never 'used up,' but rather resonate with each other. When energies come together in proper alignment, they create a wave exponentially more powerful than our individual energies could ever manifest on their own.

Introduction

The Art of Positive Thinking

On August 22-23, 2014, I set about on a profound new journey in my life. Had I known at the time that the journey would have only taken one year to accomplish, I would have been flabbergasted!

But, alas, what I have achieved is nothing short of remarkable, and even more so given the compressed time-frame in which I have accomplished it.

And we can all accomplish the same thing. Change is a process, change is hard, but look change in the face and don't fear the unknown. Look through the door of your soul and don't be afraid to walk through. A universe of possibilities lies beyond, and the first step is simply to choose to say no to fear and open the door to possibility.

I recently celebrated my one-year re-birthday, commemorating the day I chose to open the door. I told myself, on August 22-23, 2014, upon having the profound sense that I was indeed embarking on a new journey, that if that moment of Awakening were real, and not a mere specter, but if it were to hold true, then indeed August 22 would be a day I should mark in my life and celebrate as my re-birthday.

I didn't set out to specifically celebrate that date one year later, for that would have been the Ego saying, "Yep! This is going to last!" and could indeed have short-circuited the entire process.

Instead, I said, that if it did, a re-birthday party would indeed simply present itself without my Ego needing to plan one.

And so it was.

On August 22-23 of 2015, I found myself taking part in a native American PowWow ceremony at a spiritual retreat center, called The Light Center, outside of Lawrence, Kansas. Oddly, the date of that retreat itself was completely unbeknownst to my consciousness at the time. It was only after completing the FireWalk, which the PowWow triumphantly concluded with, that I became consciously aware of the date, that it was in fact the re-birthday my meta-conscious mind had planned on my behalf!

So what was this profound Awakening?

It was simply this: I woke up from the life I was living, realizing it was not the life I was born to lead, not the true Path of MySoul, and decided consciously to find the life my soul meant to manifest.

A year and one month later, I can profoundly say that I have truly, ultimately begun living the Life of My Dreams, following the true Path of MySoul.

But in order to do all of that, I had to first slay all my personal demons that were haunting me and dissolve all the barriers that were holding me back. And not just the ones I was aware of, but the subconscious forces, too!

For the past year, I had been conceptualizing and trying to pursue the life of my dreams. Now, profoundly, I am in the space where the Life of my Dreams is now pursuing me.

This has been a profound shift.

I have completed the curriculum of Self-Insight Meditation that I set out for myself. I have graduated from the School of Self Awareness, and am now fully, completely, living a life of absolute self-awareness and self-honestty. There are no boundaries remaining, separating me from the Life I am Living and the Life I was Dreaming about subconsciously. I am now fully aware of that dream, and in the Flow. I have found and am now travelling The Path of MySoul.

And you can learn how to make the same radical shifts in your life, too! I know you can. We all can.

Because I did it, and I'm nobody special. I'm just like you. And if I can do it, anybody can.

The easy-to-learn techniques in the book, can, if you apply them to you life, help you learn how to "transcend" problems instead of dwelling on them.

I have been a student of Eastern philosophy, including

Buddhism, Taosim, and Bön: the Tibetan Art of Positive Thinking for over a decade.

As Buddhist Life Coach and Motivational Speaker, I can't solve any of your problems for you. Sorry. :(

Only you can do that.

But my philosophy as a Life Coach is founded in The Tibetan Art of Positive Thinking, known as Bön, a philosophy which pre-dates Buddhism by about 15,000 years.

Bön is the original source for what has entered into modern culture as the idea that "Conscious Affects Reality" sometimes referred to as "The Secret."

Ancient Bön teachings offer specific guidelines for how this works. For readers specifically interested in learning more about Bön, I highly recommend Christopher Hansard's wonderful book simply titled: Bön: The Tibetan Art of Positive Thinking.

While this book isn't about Bön specifically, the mindset of this book is rooted in Bön's powerful belief that learning how to think from a different perspective, a Positive Perspective, has the power to change your life and change the world.

This book applies that positive perspective to a myriad of culturally-conditioned negative viewpoints which we have all been raised with. We have internalized negativity, and it has a hold on us. I propose a radically new way of viewing the culture we're living in and your own life.

Applying these principles to your life will help you see your life—your troubles as well as your triumphs—from a radically different, positive perspective.

Making that mindset shift can help you transcend whatever is currently holding you back from choosing to live the life of your dreams.

And it is just that: a choice.

We can all learn to make better choices when we internalize a new perspective, a new mindset, a new way of viewing the world from a positive perspective.

> *"Life isn't about finding yourself.
> Life's about creating yourself."*
> —George Bernard Shaw

> *"You have to let go of the life you've planned
> in order to live the life ahead of you."*
> —Joseph Campbell

*"Imagine going into the
Bookstore of your Soul
and browsing the various books.*

*Find the book that's absolutely the most
compelling to you, take it off the shelf,
and begin living it!*

*Live a life that's the most inspiring,
miraculous story you can
possibly imagine reading.*

Make that the story of your life!"

Part One

Realizing the Life of your Dreams

Don't Just Follow your Dreams... Pursue Them

To: Undisclosed Recipients
From: Tom
Date: 8/28/2015
Subject: Pursuing my Dreams

After a very rewarding 10-year career in web design, I have made the decision to transition out of the IT field, change paths completely, and transition into a new career as a Life Coach, and the term I coined is "Positive Enabler."

This has been a goal of mine since high school, and the time feels right to pursue my dreams.

On my recent cross country road trip vacation, I saw a billboard for a University that summed it up perfectly:

"Don't just follow your dreams, pursue them." That really hit home for me, and is going on my new business cards.

It has been a privilege working with each of you over the years.

In pursuit of my dreams,
Tom

A year and one week to the day of having made the decision to leave behind the security of being a successfully and lucratively self-employed web designer, I composed this email and sent it out to 75 clients who I had contact with on a weekly, if not daily, basis.

A week later, I find myself staying at The Light Center, a spiritual community 30 miles outside Lawrence, Kansas, a college town, and about an hour from Kansas City, Missouri.

It is 7 AM on a beautiful Tuesday morning, the moon setting to the West in front of me, the sun rising to the East behind me. I am sitting in full-lotus posture at my writing shrine, coffee poured, as the first words of this book come pouring out, just as I knew they would, when all of the convergent pieces of reality that have been moving into place for the past year coalesced into reality.

When all the pieces converged, the words began to flow effortlessly.

When I activated the part of my mind that asserted, "Yes, it is time! I am no longer going to think about following my dreams, I am actively going to pursue them," at that very moment, that conscious intention manifested the reality itself.

The moment I removed the final obstacle and decided to pursue my dreams, at that moment, my dreams started pursuing me.

And here I am.

Here I am.

I have come to be here, this spiritual retreat center, to live and create the space to write.

I'm writing because my spirit is incomplete when I'm not.

I am here because my spirit has been calling me to this place, or a place very much like this one, for the past 15 years.

I have been dreaming about this dream for a decade and a half, since before I started my career in web design. Throughout, the dream persisted. The further I'd gone away from it, the more incessantly it beaconed me. I could feel it calling my consciousness. I could no longer ignore the instinctual pull bringing me out of the fast-paced world that Western human ingenuity had created, to live the life my soul was born to.

The message I mean to convey with these words you are holding in your hands now is simple: everyone, including you, dear reader, has the power to manifest the life you have always dreamed of living.

> There is nothing holding any of us back, except excuses.

I know you can fill up 15 pages of journal entries with reasons for not pursuing your dreams. You can probably fill up 15 journals. I know because I did. A journal per year.

Looking back on those thoughts and ideas now, re-reading my old journals, though the entries took various forms, (exploring various incarnations of depression and anxiety, complaints about my life, minor periods of pleasure after having achieved various material successes), there was always one underlying theme, one underlying message beneath the message: I am unhappy because I am not living the life I was born to lead. I am anxious and depressed because I am afraid that I will never have the courage to take the Leap of Faith necessary to actually achieve those dreams.

A series of creative excuses led to a milieu of negative emotions and unhappiness that I coped with for over a decade. I tried various band-aids, as we all do: prescription anti-depressants, homeopathic remedies, psychoanalysis, making more money to mask the unhappiness, and a host of other activities our society prescribes to numb us to our deep, underlying feelings of incompleteness.

> The real cure for anxiety and depression is none of these. The real cure is sitting with yourself and your own thoughts.

Look inward. Turn into the mirror.

Learn how to ask yourself the hard questions, and learn how to give yourself honest answers.

I mean, the really big questions. And the really honest answers.

For example:

"Self, what would really, truly, ultimately, make you fundamentally, joyfully, ecstatically and unconditionally happy?"

I taught myself how to stop focusing on all the things I

knew were making me unhappy, and started conceiving of all the things that would actually create unconditional happiness.

The answer that I came up with was, "Unconditional Happiness? Well, actually, that's easy: Living the life of my dreams."

Next question, harder, bigger: "What does that look like?"

But wait! Don't panic!

That might not be as hard as you might think.

What if I told you that deep down, forgotten and repressed, you already have the answer, the actual, True answer, buried deep in your meta-conscious mind.

You do.

We all do.

Each of us Knows exactly why we chose to be born. The knowledge has simply been repressed through socially conditioned programming, and ignored by the You who You have been told to think that You are for as long as You can remember.

But here's the secret little secret: You are not that You.

You are consciousness.

And your consciousness has particular reasons and intentions to live the life you can chose to live.

Seeking help from therapists can be a wonderful step in the right direction. Just choose your therapist wisely. Choose one who is skillful at asking the right questions.

Of course the best therapist you can ever select is yourself.

Now, I'm not saying you should or need to do this alone. Only that you can, if you choose to. If you believe you can, then you can.

When you begin to act in accordance with your True Self, you will attract people who reflect that self, who encourage and caress your soul into becoming the best possible version of yourself.

When our thoughts, beliefs and actions align, that's the moment we begin living with intention.

And intentional living manifests other Intentional Lifers into our lives, and together, we manifest in each other the best possible versions of each of us, those parts that have been wilting away, the parts that are quite literally dying to break out of the prison where we've locked them away for so very long.

When I was in college, the thought initially came into my conscious awareness that I did not want to live in a world of 24-hour Marts, electric lights burning fossil fuels all night long, skyscrapers, pavement, and separation from Nature, our True Selves and isolation from others.

I was 21 at the time, and told I was naive and insane to think I could find a way to escape that world. I was bombarded with messages from everyone I told about my dream of transcending that world; told I would get over it eventually, and conform.

This message was pounded into my mind over and over again by almost every other human being I talked to. Years and years of being constantly and consistently bombarded by the impossibility of a thing tends to make one believe that it truly is impossible.

But, alas! Years of being constantly and consistently bombarded by the impossibility of a thing does not make that thing impossible!

But we are all brainwashed by culture into believing that dreams are largely impossible, so, like a good civilized human, I graduated college and found a job. I bought a house and lived in the suburbs.

But always, there were the undercurrents of the Other Message that I heard subconsciously, everywhere. The Other Message is there, too. We just have to learn where to find it and how to listen to it.

Tracy Chapman's song, *Fast Car,* for example.

Have you heard it? What does it mean to you?

> *"You got a fast car.*
> *Is it fast enough so we can can fly away?*
> *We gotta make a decision.*
> *Leave tonight or live and die this way."*
> —*Tracy Chapman*

That song would always give me goose bumps whenever I heard it. The message resonates quite profoundly with me.

I cannot, could not, and would not stay.

I would find a way.

If I honored my soul, I must.

So my last year in college, I had a talk with myself. It went more or less like this:

"Self, I want to escape the culturally conditioned paradigm we all live in. I don't want to participate in the infrastructure that's here now," said myself.

"Well, self, I believe we can do that, but it's going to take some time," replied my meta-consciousness.

"How long?" I asked.

"I don't know. Maybe 10 years or so," my consciousness told me.

"Yeah, let's do it."

"What's the first step?"

"I don't know yet. Let's actually do the opposite."

"Are you insane?"

"Well, you are talking to yourself, but no, not insane. Listen. Let's do the opposite. Let's do what we're told: Let's get a job, a good one. Let's really see what that's like. Let's take some time to plan our escape."

"Like Escape from Alcatraz."

"Exactly."

"They say it's impossible. That no one has escaped from Alcatraz Island."

"That's what they've been telling you, too, isn't it? Exactly that. That you can't escape. Let's choose not to believe them. But let's not let on that we don't believe them ... yet. Don't scare them! Then, when the time is right, we go."

"Why can't we go now? Right now?"

"Because I don't know how yet. We need to find a way

first. And that's going to take some time. We need to develop some skills first."

"What kind of skills?"

"I don't know. We'll find out along the way."

"Ok, self, I'm down with your idea. Let's try it."

Fast forward 15 years. Today I awoke at 7 AM to the brilliant light of dawn, dappled swatches filtering in through a canopy of trees and into my tent. True contentment and unconditional happiness washed over me for the very first time in my life.

Today I awoke to the sure and certain realization that this was Day One of my life as I intended to live it.

A toast, dear reader, to you, to all of us to Manifesting all our Dreams.

To the day we each awaken at dawn and realize we are living the life we have always imagined.

That we have Truly, Finally, arrived.

And that the path before you now is precisely the Path your Soul has known existed all along, despite everything you have ever been told.

> Here's to Trusting your Truth
> and Manifesting your Reality.

Cheers. To the day, the not-too-distant-day that only seems far away, when your real adventure begins.

"Never give up on a dream simply because of

*the amount of time it will take to achieve it.
The time will pass anyway."*
—Earl Nightingale

*"Give me six hours to chop down a tree and I
will spend the first four sharpening the axe."*
—Abraham Lincoln

*"Always make now the most precious time.
Because now will never come again."*
—Morgan Gendel

Whatever your dream, it's going to take some time and preparation.

If you haven't started yet, start right now.

Your life is ready to emerge from its chrysalis

*"We are what we think.
All that we are
arises with our thoughts.
With our thoughts,
we create the world."*
—Buddha

Imagine this mindset, because if you can imagine it, you can live it:

You live now in a state of complete openness, self-awareness and self-honesty. You know, for the very first time, the complete ecstasy of total self-acceptance and of no longer suppressing your essential self behind the illusion of the ego and culturally-conditioned inhibitions.

You have also never been more powerfully aware in your life, for you are living in a state of true flow. No illusions to cling to; Searching for the Truth of YourSoul and seeing the tip poking its head out of puffy white clouds high up in a clear blue sky that you aspire to reach.

In other words, you have never before actually felt truly alive, until today.

Rising with the sun at 7 am, awakening to a feeling of complete consciousness-cocooning confidence that you are precisely where you presently belong, the sensation being so profound that you inhale deeply, and goose bumps gently offer a pinprick caress across your arms, legs, forehead and settle down deeply into your soul.

Thoughts of snoozing longer, of lulling the body into a gentle slumber for a moment more emerge. You consider this for a brief time: The substance of that morning nap would be complete contentedness, (and imagine what dreams may come in that space!)

But alas the mind sweeps these thoughts aside for there smolders a fire in the soul to arise and awaken to the life you were born to live! To step out of the cocoon into the verdant and cool morning air, to set up one's shrine to a life of manifesting reality, and give actions to thoughts. And not just any thoughts, but the thoughts that you were put onto this world to express. The space-time-consciousness continuum has converged as the day to begin, at long last, living the life of your dreams. And knowing that your life is now ready to emerge from its chrysalis, there is no way to seriously conceive of going back to sleep.

Wouldn't that be a wonderful day? And the next day, by all reckoning, seems promising also.... For you have left all past lives, lies and illusions behind. Worries are few, and none consciously attended to. There is nothing to do that cannot be done when you are in the Flow, abiding in a land of magical manifestation, and feeling a fiercer fire in your soul to carry out your life's work with zeal than any you have ever known.

On this day your life's work begins....

"Live each day as the best possible version of today that can be conceived of."

Precognitive Feelings

If you're feeling a profound pull to start making changes in your life in order to align it with a higher purpose, know this: You are not alone.

There is a profound shift taking place, and it's beginning to spread its wings to reach more and more people with every passing day.

The first steps will manifest differently for different people. Some of us might feel compelled to quit our day jobs; others might want to leave the relationships we're currently in; still others have more of a vague notion that something about the way we've been living our lives just doesn't feel right.

These are all just ornaments of the fundamental change that's taking place. Many people are beginning to feel, in one form or another, that some way, or many ways, in which we're currently living, just feel off. We're beginning to realize that our day-to-day lives in their current form simply aren't aligning with what our souls are being called to do.

We might not know exactly what it is that we're being called to do, but in the beginning stages of this process, that's natural. The first step is realizing that what we're doing right now and the ways in which we're doing it just don't jive with our deeper sense of self.

Acknowledging that feeling is the very first step. Becoming aware of that feeling is crucial. The next step can be harder: realizing what it is we want to be doing instead.

For anyone feeling this way, realize you are not alone. There are so many of us awakening to this new reality at the same time.

> The fundamental anxiety and depression I felt was not coming from my job or from my clients, but from within.

This book grew out of my own awakening to this feeling, my own acknowledgment of it without judgment.

When I opened up to the notion that I was deeply, truly feeling this way, my soul felt compelled to explore that feeling.

Over the next year after the initial moment of awakening, I built a deeper sense of courage to reject so many elements of the life I had constructed and tied my identity to.

I was a self-employed web designer for ten years, making exceptionally good money, but deep down I was feeling a fundamental sense of anxiety and depression. At first

I thought the anxiety was solely tied to the stress of my job, deadlines, demands of clients and so forth.

To the best of my ability, (and being self employed this was easier), I altered my schedule, began taking on fewer projects and started being more proactive with setting liberal deadlines in order to combat the feeling of rush-rush-gotta-have-it-right-now that is so prevalent in our corporate culture of consumerism and immediate gratification.

These strategies helped somewhat, but didn't alleviate my underlying sense of anxiety and depression.

I realized, after some deep Self-Insight Meditation (the technique I developed and now teach, which I discuss towards the end of this book) that the fundamental anxiety and depression I was feeling was not coming from my job or from my clients, but rather, it was coming from within.

It was a result of my deep sense that I was not spending my time in a way that aligned with the reason my soul was put on Earth.

I was not meant to spend my time designing websites for other people's businesses. I was not meant to spend my life sitting behind a desk in front of a screen. I was not meant to be trading my time for money. Even though I was extremely well compensated for my time, it was no longer a trade I was willing to make.

I was meant to be spending my time doing something that manifested my soul's purpose. The underlying anxiety and depression was a result of feeling that I was not doing what I was supposed to be doing with my life.

In order to overcome those feelings, I knew I needed to spend some time with myself and truly figure out what it was I was meant to be doing. And then do it.

I've had several moments of what I consider pre-cognitive knowledge in my life. The first one I'm able to identify was a lucid dream I had when I was about 10 years old. I dreamt of a house, a very specific house, on a very specific street in my neighborhood. I remember that dream to this day, but at the time I had no idea why I was dreaming of that house.

About a year after having the dream, I met one of my childhood best friends named Nick. He lived in that house. We were best friends for several years.

The second glimpse of pre-cognition came to me when I was in college. I was majoring in English with a minor in Religious Studies, but to fulfill an elective credit, I took a class on Dreamweaver, the software used for website development. Doing some homework for that class, sitting in front of a computer, and using Dreamweaver for the first time, chills started running down my entire body. I experienced an Intuitive Knowingness that working in Dreamweaver was going to be a crucial component of my first career. I didn't know how I knew this; I simply did. My intuition really tuned in for a split second. It terrified me. I closed my book and quickly left the computer lab, terrified of that experience.

Fast forward six years, and I found myself working as a web designer, in my first real career out of college. It was a career I would stick with for a decade.

Now, the next moment of intuition is a bit harder to explain. I made the decision to leave web design for good when I realized it wasn't in line with my soul's ultimate purpose. It had served its purpose in my life. It had been a career that allowed me to earn enough income to accumulate enough savings to quit my day job and pursue my dreams.

There came a moment in my life when I became aware that the career had served its purpose. It was time to move on. This realization came to me as a flash of insight; but that was "just" Insight, not pre-cognition.

When I made the decision to leave that career, I didn't know what I was meant to do next. Or, rather, I should say, that I didn't know that I knew. But I knew I'd better think about it.

What is it that I'm meant to be doing?

So I started meditating on this. I remember that day quite clearly. I was on the back deck in the warm spring air, and set the intention for my meditation in the following way:

"Self," I said, "Let's remember the two moments of pre-cognition we've felt in our life: the dream about the house, and the knowingness about Dreamweaver. What did those feelings feel like?"

So I meditated on feeling how those feelings felt in my body, in my mind, in my conscious awareness.

And in a flash of recognition, I came to an awareness of exactly how those two feelings felt, and realized that they had both felt exactly the same.

They felt, for lack of a better word, visceral, a full-body sensation, partially characterized by goose bumps touching every cell of my skin.

I can't really put into words what they felt like. I just felt what they felt like. And I sat with that feeling.

And next I asked myself, "Ok, Self, now that we know what those feelings felt like, let's meditate on this question: Are there any other times in your life when you had that same feeling? That you weren't aware of, maybe?"

At first the answer was, "No, of course not, because if I'd had them I would have known that I ...... Oh, wait! There was that one other time, come to think about it!!"

This is the kind of deep insight that Self-Insight Meditation is exceptionally aligned with mining the mind for, bringing to the surface, shining the spotlight of conscious attention on.

In that instant, I became aware of a third instance of pre-cognition I had felt in my life. It was years ago, halfway into my web-design career. I was walking on the Riverwalk in Naperville, Illinois, when suddenly, out of the blue, I'd had a deep feeling, a deep knowing that I was meant to Teach.

Teach what? I didn't know. Something.

I was meant to be a Teacher. Not in high school or college, not that kind of teacher. A teacher who somehow, I don't know, helped people. Whatever that meant.

But that feeling very much shared the same visceral sensation that the dream about the house and the experience of being in the computer lab brought with it: a deep

Intuitive Knowingness.

So, now, sitting on my back deck, having decided to quit my day job as a web designer, I remembered having experienced this feeling years ago, though not at the time identifying it as the deep knowingness that it truly was.

Why not? Simply because at the time I'd had it, I wasn't ready to move in that direction. But now, now I was. And there was the feeling, hiding out in my sub-conscious mind, patiently waiting for the day my meta-consciousness became ready to identify it.

Now I was ready to leave my day job and pursue my real life's path ... as a teacher.

And by this time I'd begun to realize what it was I was meant to teach, how I was meant to help: by teaching these several key ideas:

1) How to build the courage to quit your day job and pursue your dreams

2) Self-Insight Meditation: how to become aware of what it is you are aware of, and learn how to follow that path

3) Be a Positive Enabler: show people the path, teach others that it's possible to live the life of their dreams. That consciousness indeed creates reality.

Those key ideas were what I was meant to point to, and to do so by living my life as an example that it can absolutely be done!

And, dear reader, the book you are now holding in your hands is one of my very first steps along that True Path of MySoul.

I am living out my life in accordance with my higher

self: doing what I was put here to do, showing others by example, that we all have the ability to live up to our potential, and live a life in pursuit of our dreams!

We can all do that. There's nothing holding any of us back except excuses.

And from that arose one of my mantras I now live by:

> *"Those who can, do.*
> *Those who can't, teach.*
> *Those who can & do & teach,*
> *change the world.*
> *Be the change."*

Live the change. We all have the potential within ourselves to identify our life's true purpose, awaken to it, and begin living a life in alignment with it.

Have you felt this way? Do you want to awaken to your true purpose?

Then you're not alone. So many of us are at this very moment waking up to that reality. I've talked to many people who feel this same way and are taking the first steps on the Path of TheirSoul towards living it.

Are you one of them?

All of us can help guide and encourage each other along this very powerful (and sometimes very scary) path.

We can walk this path together. It gets easier the more of us there are walking it.

We don't need to walk it alone.

> *"Don't just follow your dreams; pursue them."*

Now ask yourself this question, meditate on it: Have you ever had a precognitive feeling about what your soul was meant to do here in this life?

Don't be so quick to say no!

Really sit with that question and feel the answer.

I bet you have.

Far more people have had that feeling than those who've realized they've had it.

Work at realizing it. Feel what it felt like.

Self-Insight Meditation can help you to become aware of what you're currently unaware of knowing.

In your own life, could it be that any anxiety and depression you have been feeling are simply symptoms of knowing that you have a deep, purposeful meaning in life that you are not, at this moment, yet pursuing?

Could anxiety and depression simply be symptoms? Symptoms our body is using as a way of screaming at the top of its lungs, shouting: "Hey! Wake up! Wake up to your Life's True Purpose! I'm dying locked away in here!"

Find the Path of YourSoul.

Realize first what excuses you're using to hold yourself back.

Both of these goals can be achieved through Self-Insight Meditation, which can help you to identify appropriate action and develop the courage to take it.

Your meta-cognition is the part of your mind above your sub-conscious and conscious thoughts.

This is the part of your mind that is aware of what you are aware of, and can feel what you're feeling.

Self-Insight Meditation is one very helpful technique to help gently coax the meta-conscious mind out of hiding. It's scared. It's been told for so long that its Intuitions are useless.

Culture beats that message into our minds over and over and over again with its obsessive belief that we can't know anything that isn't able to be easily quantified, characterized and cross-referenced.

That is the Nature of the Box.

Meta-Cognition is the You that is Beyond the Box.

Remind yourself: There is No Box other than the one we create with our own thoughts.

> *"There was a young man who said though,*
> *it seems that I know that I know;*
> *but what I would like to see*
> *is the I that knows me*
> *when I know that I know that I know."*
>
> *—Alan Watts*

*"You've got so much to say, say what you mean
Mean what you're thinking, think anything.*

You've got to live for today, then let it go.

*If you know, then why can't you say?
You've got too much deceit, deceit kills the light
Light has to shine, I said shine light, shine."*

—*Cat Stevens*
Can't Keep It In

"Life changes at the speed of thought."

—*Robin Goff*
Founder of The Light Center

Swimming in the Flow

Cat Stevens was echoing a Buddhist philosophy when he said, "Say what you mean, mean what you're thinking." His next suggestion to "Think Anything" allows us the opportunity to really dig in and identify what it means to be in "the flow" with intention, as opposed to merely "going with it" and living your life for today.

The Buddhist-y notion that Stevens' lyrics calls to mind is perhaps best expressed this way:

Aligning and harmonizing our thoughts, words and actions is the path to eliminating suffering.

This is one way of understanding what it means to be in the flow. When our thoughts, words and actions are aligned, we create and are following a type of "personal flow" in our lives and can begin Manifesting the Life of our Dreams.

But there's a deeper flow we have access to, in which

our personal flow is only one tributary.

I believe one of the key meanings of the Greek adage, "Know Thyself" can be taken to mean: recognize what feels innately right to align your energy with. In other words, we should endeavor to teach ourselves how to orient the compass of our lives so that it aligns with the greater flow.

The life of our dreams is something we must learn how to "align with," not simply create.

It is this sense of *coming into alignment* that may be the most useful definition of "manifesting" and, by extension, "Being in The Flow"

By looking deeply within, we can become aware of what actions and skills, when we are engaging with them, allow us to feel most "in the flow."

Aspects of Being in the Flow

Most of us have already had some experience of being in the flow. So what does it feel like? Many of us have had the experience of it through some form of artistic expression that allows us to feel joy. That could be playing a musical instrument, or painting, or writing.

When we're expressing ourselves artistically, to the best of our ability in that moment, there is a sense of effortlessness.

Athletes call this space "the zone." Artists might be more inclined to call it being in the flow. But the notion is the same.

The experience of Flow shares these basic tenants:

1. Exercising all of our talents and abilities to the best of our ability in that moment.

2. Knowing thyself

3. Accepting thyself

4. Performing an activity in accordance with our inner wisdom; becoming aligned with one or more aspects of our life's purpose; participating in an activity that feels meaningful or self-expressive.

4. Letting go of the sense that we are in control. Loosening our grip on the illusion of control (and accepting uncertainty) allows us to create, play or live in a way that feels effortless. "Letting go" breaks down barriers that are holding us back.

These components together create the sense of being in flow. Another phrase for being in the flow would be, "Showing up for our lives."

Can you imagine living every moment of every day that way?

> *"In letting go of who I think I am,*
> *I can become what I might be."*
>
> —*Lao Tzu*

When every action you take during every moment of every day, seems as effortless as playing a beautiful piece of music, that's aligning your personal flow with the Universal Flow, and is the way to manifest the Life of your Dreams.

Aligning with the Universal Flow means becoming aware of the individual thread in the great web we are all weaving, and seeing how we can best apply our particular, innate skills to help weave the whole tapestry for the benefit of others, as well as ourselves.

The idea of Mutual Interdependence is also a key concept in Buddhism. Everything and every being is mutually interdependent on every other thing and being.

Every action we take vibrates the web of interconnectedness, known as Indra's Web, in the Buddhist Cosmology (discussed in a later chapter).

By achieving self-awareness and self-acceptance, we can learn to appreciate what skills and abilities are most innately strong within us, and we can learn how to apply those skills most effectively to weave the web of interconnectedness in a most effective, beautiful and skillful way.

Each of us has innate gifts and talents. We can also learn and acquire other talents in our lifetimes, through exercising intelligence, concentrated effort, attention and dedication. In fact, through exercising dedication and concentrated action, there may be very few (if any) skills that any one individual could not master.

The question we must ask ourselves is: How does learning any particular new skill best help us bring about the life of our dreams? What skills do we need to learn that will help us manifest the life our dreams?

We are in our personal flow when we align our thoughts, words and skillful actions.

Aligning our personal flow with the universal flow means understanding how we can most effectively interact with the web of interconnectedness by utilizing to the best advantage possible, all of the innate skills and abilities we possess.

When we recognize what our most innate skills and abilities are, we can then align our actions by conceiving what additional skills we may need to learn and acquire in order to best enhance and augment our innate gifts, so that we can vibrate (or weave) the web of interconnectedness in the most far-reaching way possible. That's when we become most effective with our lives: when we are applying our skills to the greatest degree possible, through a combination of honing innate skills and learning complimentary skills in order to allow our talents to shine forth most brightly.

Showing up for your life

We can only truly show up for our life when we understand and accept who we are to a sufficient level of detail so that we can clearly identify which opportunities we should show up for.

By recognizing and showing up when these opportunities present themselves, we enhance our inherent ability to weave the web of interconnectedness.

It's not just opportunities we need to show up for. Sometimes it can also be other people, whether they are teachers, students, friends, lovers, or any meaningful relationships in our lives.

Being in the flow is realizing and acting in accordance with how those relationships or opportunities are intended to manifest in a way that is the most mutually beneficial for everyone.

When we're in the flow, and show up for opportunities and people who allow us each to weave the web of interconnectedness more effectively, then we begin seeing more opportunities and people beginning to show up.

When we learn how to recognize them when they show up, and engage with them, we allow those opportunities and people to serve us and each other.

Learning how to identify the opportunities and engaging with them in the most dynamic way possible with the intention of achieving the most resonance is a useful way to understand what it means to align with the flow.

Michalangelo said the David was already in the marble. All he needed to do was chip away the unnecessary bits.

Likewise, the Life of your Dreams is already within the Flow. All we need to do is learn how to swim in it.

Concentration and wisdom are also two key tenants of Buddhism.

So, we just need to answer, wisely: What is most worth our time to concentrate on?

So, back to Cat Stevens who tells us, "Say what you mean, mean what you're thinking and think anything."

Well, only to an extent. Directed thinking is far more useful than the randomness of 'anything.' Rather, align your meaning and your thinking with your direct awareness of the part you play in the Universal Flow.

> Michalangelo believed The David was
> already in the marble.
> Likewise, the Life of your Dreams
> is already in the Flow.
> We just need to be present, to learn to swim.

And how do we do that? By "Knowing Thyself," and complimentarily, "Accepting Thyself" and thinking and behaving with intention, wisdom and acceptance as our compass.

By knowing and accepting ourselves, we can align our thoughts, words and actions in such a way to find the David within ourselves, chipping away the unnecessary bits, as well as accumulating and identifying complimentary pieces (be they other people, skills or opportunities), and learn to swim in the flow by showing up to our lives.

In this way, we can align our thoughts, words and actions with each other, (our Personal Flow) and align that with the Universal Flow, which is realizing and acting in accordance with the ways in which we can vibrate the web of interconnectedness most effectively. We are each of us just one strand of the web, yet we're all essential to the overall formation of the web itself.

Being in the Flow means correctly identifying other strands which can help us weave the fabric of the Life of our Dreams and being present to those threads when they show up in our lives.

Through cultivating awareness of ourselves and our inner work of art, we can align with the Life of Our Dreams and become the most beautiful work of art we can possibly imagine.

> *"I am an artist at living.*
> *My masterpiece is my life."*
> —*D.T. Suzuki*

*"You never change things by fighting the existing reality.
To change something, build a new model that makes the existing model obsolete."*

—R. Buckminster Fuller

"Everyone is so locked into the current way of doing things, they never see the larger picture or other, more responsible and efficient possibilities.

It is a total shift in intent than what we have today."

— Peter Joseph

Part Two

Transcending Cultural Conditioning

The Force of Conscious Intention

While people debate whether we have yet reached the tipping point of global warming, I feel very profoundly with every fiber of my being that there is a different tipping point we have already eclipsed. We have already begun the transformation of civilization into a new state of conscious awakening that does not merely solve, but transcends, all of the confluent crises our civilization is on a collision course with.

There is a profoundly powerful new faith-based-spirituality that has emerged into our cultural consciousness. It is rooted in the dawning awareness that consciousness creates reality.

If you can dream it, you can do it.

The idea that consciousness itself is truly the fundamental substance of the universe has been sown into the soil of cultural awareness in too many ways to ignore any longer. And the seeds have already begun to sprout.

> Culture may try to bury this idea
> without realizing it's a seed
> that sprouts in fertile minds.

The idea is simple: that consciousness creates reality, that as individuals and as a civilization, it is our collective and individual consciousnesses that manifest reality itself.

The idea that consciousness creates reality is ... well ... what is consciousness afterall?

How do you like this for a working definition of consciousness? Consciousness is....

"It's an energy field, created by all living beings. It surrounds us and penetrates us; it binds the universe together."
—*Obi-Wan Kenobi*

Consciousness is the fundamental fabric of reality.

It is the age-old idea of the Ether.

It is the Higgs Field that quantum physicists propose.

It is the basis for the Unified Field theory Stephen Hawking looks for.

It is *The Force*, for lack of a better word. And there may truly be no better word.

It is the Power of Intention; It is The Secret, to use the vernacular.

It is the Way (or The Flow), to invoke Eastern Taoism.

To be clear, this power is not new. The human conception of it is nothing new. It's been understood for thousands of years, just forgotten, repressed, in favor of a culture contaminated by the sickness of ego-driven greed.

> Here is my definition of ego-driven greed: the exploitation of the needs of the many to serve the needs of the few, or the one.

And that is the sickness, the cancer, which has been the fundamental infection suffered by Western Civilization for the past 5,000 years or more.

But fundamentally, we have reached the tipping point where the knowledge of this fundamental truth has finally been re-awakened in the minds of Western Civilization. It is now that healing begins. It is now that the world changes.

So why is *The Force* perhaps the best word to describe the new perception of the universal "Secret" that consciousness creates reality?

Because our culture is extremely science-oriented. It has rejected religion out-of-hand; it has thrown the baby out with the bath water, faith out with dogma.

Science Fiction therefore becomes the crack in the cultural egg through which this idea sows its seeds, and brings us into the light of awakening.

Further, illustrating that what we think as a culture and as individuals does become reality, dozens of lists have been compiled (which you can find easily through a quick Google search) of several hundred pieces of daily technology that have come into existence in Science Fact that were first dreamed up in Science Fiction, specifically, *Star Trek* and *Star Wars.* You see, many of the Apple Techies are Trekkies, and so the iPad, iPhone, even email, etc., etc., are rooted fundamentally in sci-fi based technologies. Science fiction fans who have become techies pioneer new technologies based on what they have been dreaming up for a half century.

Anything we can imagine has the potential to become the reality of the future.

Star Wars has significant spiritual underpinnings. The Jedi are based on Taoist Masters, and *The Force* is based on the The Flow.

And The Flow (or The Way) is the basis for what we think of today as The Secret, or the Power of Intention. People who are "One with the Way" we call "Master Manifesters."

Consciousness affects Reality.

The idea that positive thinking creates a positive reality, is rooted in the Ancient Tibetan philosophy of Bön, which pre-dates Buddhism by as much as 15,000 years.

It has been passed down through the millennia in a milieu of various forms, from Buddhism to the original, uncorrupted teachings of Jesus, just to cite two more common examples.

And finally, we have reached the tipping point where this idea has infiltrated culture to a great enough extent that as a civilization, I believe our paradigm is spring-loaded with willingness and readiness to begin acting in accordance with it. Indeed, many of us already have.

And there are more and more of us awakening everyday, as ideas like this become more omnipresent in real life, and online, on places like Elephant Journal, Facebook and YouTube and all other forms of social media that are manifesting this meme.

And as this meme becomes more deeply believed by culture as a whole, and acted upon by culture at large, that's when the world changes. When each of us starts to realize that our consciousness creates reality, there can be no motivations that could possibly linger for living lives that are not allowing us to experience the true nature of life: Purpose, meaning, intention, love.

> The flower of Awakening is ready to bloom
> in the minds of the humans living on this
> tiny blue dot in the vast cosmos,
> bound together by consciousness.

That is the new faith-based spirituality that has emerged into our cultural worldview, and it has the power to truly, fundamentally, change the world and culture as we know it.

There are too many instances of this idea, too many different manifestations of it, from *Star Wars* to spiritual gurus like Alan Watts and Adyashanti; from mainstream books like *"What the Bleep Do We Know?"* to *"The Secret"* for this fundamental truth, this Force, to be ignored.

From suburban soccer moms who have read, or at least heard of *"The Secret"* on Oprah, to spiritual seekers who align with the burgeoning rise of Buddhism in the West, the seeds of this fundamentally profound and powerful truth have been planted in one form or another in the minds of the majority of Western Civilization.

And this is The Force that has the power of maneuvering the rudder on the ship of civilization we are sailing, this spaceship Earth, that's headed directly on a collision course with Global Warming, economic collapse and a myriad of other cultural problems poised to converge.

The Force to change the direction of culture and avoid this collision has impregnated itself into our cultural consciousness.

The seeds are planted and have already begun to sprout. The conditions are right. The flower of awakening is ready to bloom in the minds of the humans living on this tiny blue dot in the vast cosmos, bound together by consciousness.

New World in the Morning

Perhaps you have seen documentaries such as *Zeitgeist* or *The Eleventh Hour*.

These documentaries, and others like them, are beating the war drum about all the confluent problems Western Civilization has created for itself, manifested primarily out of a mindset infected by the sickness of greed.

The Eleventh Hour, narrated by Leonardo DiCaprio (based on a book by the visionary political and spiritual teacher Thom Hartman, titled *The Last Hours of Ancient Sunlight),* takes as its subject the rampant expanse of the fossil fuel-burning industry which is very rapidly consuming the life blood of the Earth herself. To be clear, burning fossil fuels is not the core problem; this is merely an ornament of the underlying disease of greed running rampant in our culture. It's not the activity that's the problem, but the mindlessness of addiction to wanting ever more and more and never, ever being satisfied.

The documentary, *Zeitgeist*, more profoundly, identifies not just one, but several key ornaments of confluent crises which are threatening to converge as a result of our toxic mindset.

There are numerous documentaries all beating this mother drum, announcing to everyone, shining the light of a new dawn, onto all the problems that are emerging into the cultural consciousness.

I believe it is inherently a good thing that this drum is being beaten, but to use the age-old adage, there is no use beating a dead horse.

(Side note: the metaphor of beating a dead horse originated in book, *Crime and Punishment* by Fyodor Dostoyevsky when the main character has a dream in which a dead horse is being beaten. The main character, Raskolnikov, wakes up to realize how useless and futile such an activity is.)

I believe we are coming to a point now where the message of how bad things are becoming has infiltrated the cultural consciousness to such a degree that continuing to beat the war drum is analogous to beating a dead horse.

The problem with explaining all the problems is that it keeps us focusing on the problems and not the solutions.

It also paralyses us into thinking, "This shit's gotten so real, damn!, no solutions can possibly be possible!"

Both documentaries I mentioned above spend the first three-fourths of their screen-time discussing the problems, and only the last thirty minutes contemplating any solutions.

The problems must be identified, yes.

But after identification, we must move on the focus on solutions.

And there are solutions.

And the trend I see emerging in society now is the realization that it's becoming time to focus on the solutions, not the problem.

Realizing the problems merely serves as the initial stage in awakening, as individuals and as a civilization.

But true awakening is achieved when our cultural consciousness begins to focus its energy primarily on solutions, not problems.

This is the trend I see emerging.

This is what this book is about.

So, where do solutions start?

They start in the hearts and minds of people like you and me.

> Solutions begin in the hearts and minds of people like you and me, who have awakened to the realization that we are not, currently, living the Life of our Dreams but rather dying as slaves to a life others have told us to lead.

When each of us starts living the Life of our Dreams, then and only then, can we change the world.

Change starts with you. From within. One person at a time. One person choosing to do things differently.

As more and more individuals learn to align with the flow, we begin to weave together a much different web of interconnectivity.

That web starts to vibrate in an entirely different way, one that's more in line with virtuous activity.

And this has the power to change the entire world.

> *"I've been happy lately*
> *Thinking about the good things to come*
> *And I believe it could be*
> *Something good has begun*
>
> *I've been smiling lately*
> *Dreaming about the world as one*
> *And I believe it could be*
> *Someday it's going to come."*
>
> —*Cat Stevens*

Who do I want to Be when I Wake Up?

*"Ask not,
'What do I want to be when I Grow Up?'
But rather,
'Who do I want to Be when I Wake Up?' "*

The combination of compassion and action has been welling up within us for a while now, and it's reached a tipping point.

For me, that tipping point is manifested in the ideas contained in the book you're reading right now.

Fundamentally, there is one underlying kernel of truth that, if you take away nothing else from my ideas, I would want you to come away with having internalized: *Do not do what you're told simply because you're told to do it.*

It is our responsibility, as thinking human beings, as intelligent life forms, to hold up to the light of analytical thinking, to ask:

Why are we being told to do the things we are told to do?

Who are we being told by?

And, at a higher level, are you, as an individual, only doing the things you are doing because you've been told to do them?

Do these things feel right to you?

Do they Align with the true Path of YourSoul?

The way you live your life—the things you are doing every day, every single day, the patterns, the routines, even the breaks from routine, the vacations you choose to take—are those things undertaken of your own conscious will, or do you do them because those are the things you're told are acceptable, proper, good, to do.

Have you questioned this truth yourself?

How deeply?

Now I don't mean any of this to sound too harsh, like I'm blaming you for not questioning your life. I'm not at all.

We are born and raised in a culture that specifically teaches us not to question, not to express our individuality, not to lead our lives, not to think for ourselves.

Think of it in this way: In our culture we, of course, have artists, musicians, free-thinkers, hippies, but I want you to think now how each of those vocations, some to a higher degree than others, have extremely negative connotations associated with them.

Our culturally-induced consciousness and morality, through our media, highlights the cases of professional musicians who have overdoses or have seen their lives ruined by extreme indulgences.

Starving artists, too, have the stigma of being poor, dirty, good-for-nothing Rastafarians.

Our culture demonizes them, places them outside the acceptable life choices we are told to make.

At the same time, we're raised being told that we can do whatever we want, be whatever we want.

(Not, whoever, mind you, but whatever. This implies you must tie your identity to your career. Rubbish!)

> The underlying assumption is that your identity is intrinsically tied to what you get paid to do.

The subtext is that you can be whatever you want, so long as that you make something of yourself... something acceptable. And the cultural concept of what is acceptable has a very narrow definition: to be something when you grow up means to have a high-paying job. Run ever faster on the Hedonistic Treadmill of consumerism.

So, what do you want to be when you grow up?

Acceptable answers are of course, architect, engineer, firefighter, even ballerina will do for a young idealistic child, but still, notice a pattern? Even a Ballerina is a job. The underlying assumption is that your identity is intrinsically tied to what you get paid to do.

But now that you're an adult, you have the mental

capacity to ask yourself that question again, and ask it correctly. Realize that who you are doesn't have to be defined by your job.

A friend just asked me, "Why would I want to grow up at all?" A very poignant question. Growing up has some real negative associations with it, doesn't it?

What does it mean to grow up? Well, it means precisely this: To have a job, to most likely be married, to have a house and a car.

"What do you want to be when you grow up?" translates this way: What method of employment do you think you would least dislike, which will pay you enough money, so that you can achieve the things that you are not allowed to fundamentally question the necessity of.

So by answering the question, it forces me to accept the unquestioned, underlying assumption that I have to have a job to afford the car I'll need to get to it and the house I'll need to sleep at when I'm not working at it.

Ironically, answering this question, is not at all thinking about your life. It's giving away the power to create your life, surrendering your life to society, which has already decided, in broad strokes, what you are going to be in your life: basically, a cog in the wheel keeping our society running.

So that's why I refuse to answer that question. I want to take back the power of my life.

I want to fundamentally question if I even want most of the things culture tells me I need.

Knowing yourself, and analyzing the trajectory of

your life, and figuring out how to Pursue the True Path of Your Dreams is the first and primary question to apply your conscious attention to.

So let's rephrase the question:

Who do you want to be when you wake up?

"If you really like what you're doing, it doesn't matter what it is, you can eventually become a master of it. And then you'll be able to charge a good fee for whatever it is.

Do that and forget the money, because, if you say that getting the money is the most important thing, you will spend your life completely wasting your time.

You'll be doing things you don't like doing in order to go on living, that is to say, go on doing things you don't like doing."

—*Alan Watts*

"There is no scarcity of opportunity to make a living at what you love; there's only scarcity of resolve to make it happen."

—*Wayne Dyer*

Change starts with every individual choosing a different path.

The path (so far) less traveled.

> "Two roads diverged in a wood, and I
> I took the one less traveled by,
> And that has made all the difference."
>
> —Robert Frost

> "I met a man who had a dream
> he had since he was 20.
>
> I met that man when he was 81.
>
> He said, "Too many folks just
> wait until the morning."
>
> Don't they know tomorrow never comes?
>
> I, myself, don't talk about a
> New World in the Morning.
>
> New World in the Morning?
>
> That's today."
>
> — Roger Whittaker

The Sickness of Greed

My worldview has matured over the years, as all of ours do.

Far from the young and naïve college student who dreamed of merely escaping our corrupt culture, I have now come to believe, profoundly, deeply, that we have created a beautifully complex, robust, dynamic civilization.

We can transmit ideas almost at the speed of thought across the globe via the magic of the Internet. We can transport ourselves at the speed of sound across those same distances.

> *"Any sufficiently advanced technology is indistinguishable from magic."*
> —Arthur C. Clarke

The dreams we can achieve using the miraculous-seeming technologies Western ingenuity has conceived of is truly astonishing and profound.

We have built a civilization that has transcended Maslow's Hierarchy of Needs.

We have the technology to meet and exceed the basic needs of every single human on the planet.

We live in a world where hunger need not exist.

In America, we waste, by some estimates, at least 50% of the food we produce.

Grocery stores select only the most perfect-looking produce and discard the rest.

Unsold food goes into dumpsters at the end of the day from restaurants and grocery stores alike. And in many municipalities, laws are in place preventing those foods from being given to the homeless. It's patently absurd. A good lawyer could quite literally devise a way for this level of absurdity to be patented in our legal system.

The food we waste is more than enough to feed every person on the planet.

The technology is there.

The motivation simply isn't.

Our motivation is for profit, solely that.

Our civilization is miraculous.
Let's do our damndest to keep it.
Let it be subsumed no longer
by the sickness of greed.

Let's change our mindset before it really is too late.

Before we go the way of Rome, or Atlantis, or any other sufficiently advanced civilization from History or Mythology.

Let's not throw the baby out with the bath water.

Let's change our mindset before it's too late.

That's all that needs to change.

Just our mindset.

It's so simple.

Changing our mindset starts here, now, with you and me.

> *"The white man is corrupted*
> *by the sickness of greed."*
>
> *—The Last of the Mohicans,*
> *1992 film adaptation*

Civilization is a tool

We live in an amazingly, profoundly advanced civilization with astonishingly advanced technology that really has delivered on all of the promises that the most altruistic, utopian visionaries suspected it could.

When the Industrial Revolution first began, the promise it held was that machines could drastically reduce the need for physical labor and toil. If machines did all of our work for us, humans would only have to work one day a week, and leave all of the other days free from strife.

But what have we seen instead?

We use our machines to accomplish the same tasks more quickly, to accomplish even more that we had previously dreamed possible.

Then the Intellectual Revolution occurred, which brought computers.

It may cause a mid-life crisis! 57

And again, the promise entered the fringes of the cultural consciousness: that computers would allow us to get all of our work done in a third of the time, or even less.

But the trend repeated itself: as soon as more time became available, culture devised to use all the newly-available time to dream up even more things to dream about and occupy its time developing.

So, we have created a world in stark opposition to the one visionaries dreamed of. In today's world, we have less time than ever. We are living busier, faster, more "productive" lives, constantly doing, producing, growing, consuming.

But nevertheless, the potential of promise has been achieved, if not fulfilled.

> Intuitive knowingness points toward Truth.

We do have the tools and resources to accomplish far more than we need to accomplish in a far more condensed timeframe than the Earth revolves around the sun.

Stated more clearly: in the 24-hour period we call a day, we are accomplishing more work than might previously have been completed in, perhaps, an entire year. These timeframes are arbitrary. There may very well be actual studies that show exactly how many "technology-free-man-hours" are being expended in every 24-hour period.

But I'm not interested in studies. I'm interested in Intuitive knowingness pointing toward Truth.

Who would argue that we are accomplishing an obscene amount per day, aided by digital computers, mechanical machines, fossil fuels and a seemingly limitless wellspring of human innovation, achievement, misdirected motivation and an underlying restlessness and greed to do ever more, to have always more, to perpetually grow, without respite or reprieve.

The so-called free time that we do have (weekends) are spent by most of us frantically shopping, surfing the Internet, watching television—in short, doing almost anything except relaxing. We feel an overwhelming, underlying sense of anxiety, restlessness and guilt when we actually do take time to relax, sit down, and do, literally, nothing.

When's the last time you sat on your front porch sipping a glass of lemonade waving to your neighbors doing the same?

Can you even imagine doing that on a Saturday morning?

Imagine that setting. How would being there, in that place of calm, slow morning relaxation make you feel?

If you're like most of the rest of the Western World, you would spend most of that time worrying about what you had to do during the rest of the day and the next week. And with that mindset, we are fundamentally missing the point.

Civilization has enslaved us all into a state of constant worry and anxiety that we are not doing quite enough, promoting the belief that we never can be doing quite enough.

So we take anti-anxiety pills. And anti-depressants.

What's wrong with this picture?

A lot, actually, and we all know it.

Admitting we have a problem is the first step to changing.

The fact is, we have created a civilization of unprecedented abundance. None of us, the 7 billion people on the planet, need ever worry about having our basic needs met: food, water, shelter, clothing.

Why, then, are there children starving in America? In Africa? In South America? Everywhere.

Because we are greedy, and hoarding all the food.

Because 1/2 of all the food you buy at the grocery store goes in one end and out the other.

Into the fridge, and a week later into the trash.

Or into our mouths in the morning and out our asses at night.

We don't need to eat as much as we do.

We don't need to waste anything.

But we do. Of course we do.

And that's why there are starving children.

It has nothing to do with scarcity.

It has to do with the disease of greed that is afflicting our civilization like a calcified cancer, the Black Death of the modern era.

And all of us are infected. All of us.

Including me. And you, too. To one degree or another, we are all guilty as charged.

No one's going to lock us up in a prison for crimes against humanity. That's the easy way out.

The punishment I'm proposing is much more severe,

much harder for most of us to accept.

The punishment should fit the crime.

The punishment is simple.

Change.

Change ourselves. Change our mindset.

Change starts with every individual choosing to make different choices.

This amazingly wonderful, miraculous civilization we have created is being abused by all of us who have inherited this life of plenty.

For anyone reading this book, anyone with disposable income enough to buy it, none of us have anything, not really, to worry about.

We aren't going to starve.

We aren't going to die of thirst.

We aren't going to get eaten by a predator.

Do you know the story of the Nobel Peace Prize?

Alfred Nobel is best known for creating an endowment fund that annually awards a large monetary allowance to innovators working for peace and positive change in the world.

Nobel created this fund in the hope that he would be best remembered for his altruism. Why?

Because he also invented dynamite.

He invented it as a tool, to assist in construction of new bridges, roads, etc.

But as soon as he saw the destructive power of dynamite, he knew humanity would corrupt it into a dreadful weapon.

The same basic story is true of Nuclear Power. It has the tremendous potential to provide energy and electricity.

Of course its most notorious use is for a weapon of war.

It's the same story over and over again, throughout the annals of history.

Powerful tools being used as weapons of mass destruction.

Civilization itself follows the exact same pattern.

The tremendously advanced global technological infrastructure we have created has fundamentally delivered on its promise to free us all from starvation and strife. We all have all our basic needs met, and none of us need give our basic needs a second thought. Or a first one, for that matter.

We have everything that we have ever wanted.

Our glorious civilization has gifted that to us.

We were all born with a silver spoon.

Only we don't realize it.

Some people say that "Technology will save us!"
But the fact is: it already has.
We just need to realize it.

And we need to use that silver spoon as a tool, instead of choking on it.

And the change starts on an individual level, when we each start living our lives differently.

So, how do we change?

The first step is so ridiculously easy a child could do it. Maybe better said, only a child can do it.

Change your focus.

Spend more time everyday focusing on the ways in which you have absolute, complete and utter contentment in your life, instead of the ways in which you are grasping for more (which is what most of us do most moments of most days).

Spend more time focusing on the positive instead of the negative. As a culture, we are really profoundly brainwashed into focusing on the negative. We focus on what we don't have, and on all the problems we think we have. We spend an enormous amount of mental energy focusing on these areas.

And we're stuck in that thought-loop that is constantly self-perpetuating.

It's a treadmill of thinking. And a hamster wheel.

As long as we keep running, it keeps spinning.

Jump off!

Using the Tool Wisely

It's pretty incredible that Aborigines in Australia can survive a months-long walkabout through the parched desert interior of the island, bringing no food or water with them.

From the outsider's perspective, the interior of the island is a waterless, lifeless expanse inhospitable to human life.

But the Aboriginal tribesmen and women are so in tune with their own environment that they are able to find water tables beneath the desert surface. They can quite literally sense the water, though, by all appearances, there is simply none to be found.

Sound miraculous?

Now imagine a variation on this story....

Imagine being a tourist in a large modern western metropolis. Wandering down paved city streets with skyscrapers towering above your head, it's incredibly easy to find water when you need it, and find food whenever you want it.

Water is everywhere. You just have to know how to look for it.

An Aborigine coming to Chicago would have no clue where to look for water in the pavement-encrusted city. He would be used to digging in the sand and sucking water out of the desert through a straw. There's no way he would know to walk into a building, up to a metal cube protruding from a wall, apply pressure to a button labeled "Push" in order to initiate a stream of water from a spout.

We call this simple technology a water fountain.

To an Aborigine, it would be impossible to comprehend. Magic.

But both Aborigines and Western Man are perfectly knowledgeable about their own environments, and know where to go to find what they need.

It's as simple as that.

Just like water from a fountain, our Western Civilization, despite all its corruption, greed and toxic mentalities, provides everything that we could possibly ever need. Just like the desert does for an Aborigine.

The problem is, we're so fixated on what we don't have, that we have become completely blind to all the miraculous things that we do have.

It's time to change our mindset and start focusing on the positive.

Our mindset is so calcified and, by this time, generationally conditioned to focus on the negative, that this subtle shift seems to be something that's going to be incredibly hard to do.

But only thinking makes it so.

See, again, we're focusing on the negative. "Oh, it's going to be so hard to change!"

No, it's not.

It's only going to be hard to change so long as you keep thinking about the paradigm you're trying to transcend.

Stop thinking about how to change, and start thinking about how to be different.

It's not a change.

It's a being, a doing.

Change is hard.

Doing is easy.

We do it all the time.

We just don't realize that we're doing it all the time.

We're just doing the wrong things, all the time.

Identifying the problem is the real first step.
So what's the problem?

> The problem is we're wasting all our mental energy focusing on the negative, the I-can't-do-this-because-of-this-thing mentality.

Stop doing that.

Oh, what's that your mind is telling you right now as you were reading those words?

That you can't stop doing that because of ... why?

Forget why.

There is no why.

Stop letting your mind make up excuses.

And stop believing them.

Your mind is lying to you!

"Abundance is not something we acquire. It is something we tune into."

—*Wayne Dyer*

The Problem with Fossil Fuels

The biggest problem with fossil fuels is not global warming.

It's that we are using them irresponsibly.

It took the Sun millions of years to generate all the energy that billions of plants and animals aggregated into life, and decomposed into what we now, millions of years later, take for granted in the form of fossil fuels.

And what it took nature millions of years to create, we will burn through in a mere couple centuries (if that, if we continue at our current pace.)

> *"We are living on the
> last hours of ancient sunlight."*
> —Thom Hartman

All of this is true. But instead of focusing on the problems, it's time now to focus on beauty, and from the place of appreciating beauty, we must learn that what we have is worth preserving.

And only from that mindset can we possibly begin to materialize solutions.

If we don't realize that what we have is worth keeping, then we will continue on our collision course with destruction and let it all collapse.

So the work ahead of us now as a civilization is to truly appreciate what an amazingly beautiful civilization we have created. It has flaws sure.

But it's a real work of art.

We have manifested a technology indistinguishable from magic that allows us to zip from one side of the globe to another, literally at the speed of desire.

If we desire to go to Ireland, or Myanmar, we can go.

We have manifested a world that caters to our every whim. The more we cater to them, the more we desire, and the more we feel like we need to cater to the next level of desire.

Not only can we travel across the globe, we can leave it in ships (primitive, yes, by Stark Trek standards),

We have GPS because we are able to tell time to seven decimal places. We invented time. We tell it what to do.

We also invented nuclear power.

We are also feeding 7 billion humans every day.

Think we aren't?

We're not doing it gracefully, but make no mistake: we are.

People are hungry, not eating enough, starving, poor, destitute, but we are absolutely feeding 7 billion people. If we weren't, then the population would not keep increasing. But it is. Every day, our population grows.

The fact that people are starving and poor is a result of greed and ignorance, not a limitation of our technology.

We, as a species, have manifested a fundamentally magical civilization of mind-boggling technological complexity.

We have mapped the universe to see not only outside our solar system, not only outside out galaxy, but into the supercluster of galaxies to which we belong. It's called Laniakea, a Hawaiian word translating into English as "Immeasurable Heaven."

We have been able to see that the Universe consists of strands of interconnected strings of galactic clusters that mimic the formations of the individual molecules of wispy algae floating in an immeasurably vast ocean.

And our whole universe is like one algae plant in that ocean.

We know all of this.

We have learned all of this by applying the power of our unfathomably powerful intellect.

Life has been on Earth for 4 billion years. Ancient forests that covered the globe, geologists can describe in great detail, and they know somehow, the size of the trees in those forests. They were twice as big as the Redwoods in modern-day California.

And forests like that covered our planet 3 billion years ago for an incredibly long time, maybe a billion years.

That's where our fossil fuels come from!

We know all of this.

Fossil fuels are a gift from the childhood of the Earth herself.

It took 3 billion years for Earth to manifest this gift for us.

The worst possible thing we can do with the gift Earth has bestowed on us is to use it irresponsibly.

So what does *responsible* look like?

> Responsible means using an amount of fuels each year that matches our need, and not our desires. Responsible means fueling the quality of our lives, not their excessive gluttony.

Responsible as a society means the same as responsible as an individual: holding up all your desires and perceived wants, to the light of thoughtful consideration:

Do I really need this?

Do I really want this?

Will having this thing create more misery for me or anyone else?

Will this thing I think I want bring me happiness, or just pleasure?

Is it the thing itself I actually want, or do I just want to want it?

When I have it, will I be less happy, or more happy than how happy I thought I was while I was on the perpetual quest to get it?

Do I know what real, true, meaningful happiness is?

These are the questions our civilization needs to be asking itself on a global level as well as from an individual perspective, and everywhere in between.

As individuals, what do we need to actually better ourselves? To become a better person?

As a civilization, what do we need to actually become a more enlightened culture?

Technology, even fossil fuels, when utilized responsibly, and effectively, has the abundant ability to better our lives in ways that we have barely begun imagining. Largely, it's because we are obsessed with telling ourselves how 'not good enough' everything is, and how we always need it to be better.

Choking on the Silver Spoon

*"Be careful what you wish for ...
you will get it."*

What do you think is the single most phenomenal thing about the astonishingly advanced civilization we have created for ourselves?

The Internet?
Plane travel?
Space travel?
Solar power?
No, none of these.

The single most phenomenal aspect inherent to the astonishingly advanced civilization we have created is its ability to completely and utterly satisfy every single little whim and desire we all have on a regular basis.

Hungry? You can find a McDonalds without looking for one.

If you look a little harder and you happen to be in Kansas City where I've lived for the past three years, you can find a myriad of healthful, or even raw food choices, such as places with fun names like, *Cafe Gratitude* or *Eden Alley* or more to the point, *Füd*.

None of us will ever go without.

No cash? No problem. Use a credit card.

> Your wish, says the genie of Mother Culture, is my command!

Pay with cash, pay with debt (credit), it matters not. You can have every little thing that your heart desires.

Bored? How about 4,000 TV channels. Not enough?

How about Internet-streaming content like Netflix or Amazon?

The sky truly is no limit.

Simply say what you want, pay the genie, and pop goes the weasel. Whatever you want. Whatever you can imagine. And it manifests. Imagine that!

Truly, truly, astonishing and amazing.

Can you imagine how a cave man would feel entering into our world?

No need to hunt, no need to gather, find water, sleep in the darkness frightened by wild wolves or hungry lions.

It is all, simply, easily, effortlessly provided.

No struggle, no strife. It's all available. Here and now.

With nothing more than a moment's thought.

Astonishing.

How many times do we actually stop to think about how miraculous that is?

Now, let's take that to the next level.

What do you really want?

Do you really, truly, actually want to sit there and numb your mind with TV?

Or fatten your belly with food?

Or addle yourself with drink?

What do you really want?

That might be the absolute hardest question to answer.

But make no mistake, if you actually, truly think about what it is that you really want, the astonishingly sophisticated culture we have created can provide it … as surely as if it were a McDonald's cheeseburger.

Beliefs like these are already imbedded in our cultural consciousness, taking on New Agey-type names like, "The Law of Attraction" or "The Secret" or "Manifest Your Reality," and so on.

We need to be careful of these ideas if we continue to approach them from the toxic mindset of greed. There are people out there actively trying to manifest piles and piles of money. And succeeding. And making all kinds of trouble for everyone else at the same time.

So, how is this possible?

The so-called Power of Intention can be explained without any need whatsoever for spiritually vague ideas.

Personally, I prefer spiritually sophisticated ideologies that explain these phenomenon more accurately, such as the Buddhist concept of "Indra's Web," but for the moment, let's take a less esoteric route and explain The Power of Intention in a very straight forward, rational way that even the most ardent scientifically-minded reductionist atheist can appreciate.

The Law of Attraction is, in this paradigm, simply an emergent property of a sufficiently sophisticated civilization.

Our minds work by seeing and identifying patterns. It's simply a skill we have developed out of sheer survival-of-the-fittest evolution.

The cave man who identified the pattern of the moving leaves at the edge of the clearing as a predator was able to choose fight-or-flight.

The cave man who ignored the pattern of the moving leaves probably got eaten by whatever it was that pounced on him.

Now, extrapolate that ability to being able to see much more sophisticated patterns. Stock market patterns, for example.

Highly successful stock brokers simply see patterns in the market first, before anyone else, act on their awareness of those patterns and make millions of dollars.

Pattern recognition. That's all it is.

A sophisticated mind learns which patterns to pay attention to and which to ignore. And the mind does so in accordance with whatever it's looking for.

If you desire a million dollars, identify patterns in the market and trade skillfully in accordance with those patterns.

If what you want is an eye-candy, trophy-style short-term-life-partner, identify patterns that allow you to find where that person is, and patterns that allow you to modify your behavior to attract that person. It's really that simple.

Sadly, so many members of our culture confuse their actual desires with these artificial ornaments.

What do they think they really want?

Money. And Sex. And Food. And a big screen TV. And a house in the suburbs.

If that's really all you want, it's pretty easy to achieve these things by simply studying the patterns that the most successful people employ to achieve these ends.

Now why is this so easy?

Because that's the infrastructure that our society has set up. Society encourages us to want these things, and makes it relatively easy to achieve them as long as we conform to the correct patterns.

Personally, I have achieved all of these things relatively easily, by simply behaving in accordance with the patterns I identified as pre-requisite on this path.

But when I had achieved these things, I realized, these things were not at all what I really wanted.

I was simply conforming to what society told me I should want.

Now, look, you might not like this, but if you're reading

this book, you are relatively affluent. You are, generally speaking, a member of the so-called privileged class of society.

I'm not saying we're the 1% here, (which is actually more like the 0.00001%), but we do hold a place of privilege in our culture.

We're well-educated, intelligent (you can read, can't you? Then you're more highly trained in intelligence than 99.999999% of every hominid that has ever walked the Earth), and highly sophisticated.

Can you know the difference between a Merlot or a Budweiser? Yes, of course you do.

Could a caveman? No. They are both merely fermented drinks to him.

And you can manifest either a Merlot and a Budweiser in a maximum of 30 minutes by getting in your car and driving to the store.

Could a caveman? Of course not. It would have taken a full year of the growing cycle, harvest and fermentation to achieve the result of an intoxicating brew.

Are you seeing my point here?

Living in America, we can manifest anything. Anything at all that we desire.

Satisfying desires (manifesting your own reality) is an emergent property of the sufficiently sophisticated civilization we have achieved.

We were all born with the Silver Spoon.

And we're all choking on it.

Now what do I mean we're choking on it?

Simply this:

We're slaves to immediate gratification.

And for the most part, we only desire what we're told we should desire by Mother Culture.

But make no mistake about this:

Our sufficiently sophisticated civilization is something right out of science fiction. It can give us anything we want, anything at all. Anything we can imagine, we can have.

And there was no need for New Age spirituality. No need to invoke The Law of Attraction or Faith of any kind. It is simply an emergent property of our civilization.

Now, back to the fundamental question:

What do you *really* want?

And what's standing in your way?

Nothing but excuses. And that fact that you've never really thought about it.

Because you've spent your whole life up until now choking on the silver spoon.

> What's standing in your way?
> Nothing but excuses.

The fact that we abuse this phenomenal gift culture has given us is nauseatingly unacceptable in my opinion.

And even worse is that our culture is abusing us by not even presenting the truth: Yes, you absolutely can have everything that you want.

Not the things it wants you to have: big screen TVs, capitalist propaganda, material goods, ticky-tacky houses, etc. Is that what you really want?

If it is, why are you reading this book?

Culture was created by us, by humans.

Culture is a tremendously powerful tool.

And we need to learn how to utilize the tremendously sophisticated power it has rewarded us with in return. And we need to learn how to use that power appropriately, effectively, efficiently and maturely.

And if we don't, it's going to collapse.

It's going to rebel against us if we continue abusing it.

Let's call that Human Colony Collapse Disorder.

Zeitgeist and *The Eleventh Hour* have told us that story.

The real question is what do we need to do to prevent it from happening?

We need to wake up!

"Everything changes when you start to emit your own frequency rather than absorbing the frequencies around you. When you start imprinting your intent on the universe rather than receiving an imprint from existence."

—*Evolver Social Movement
Facebook Community*

Part Three

Awakening to your Higher Self

Who are you?
Are you ready to find out?

You are, at this very moment, exactly what you have put your intention, motivation and desires into. You are who you have been imagining yourself to be all along.

Now, the important question, is that who you want to be?

Is the identity you have created for yourself (your personality) in alignment with your Essential Self?

And if the answer is no, who do you want to be, really?

What do you want to put your energy into?

When you consider these bigger questions, you may find that many of the things in your life you have been using to define your identity, your reality, are not actually aligned with the person you are or want to become.

Are your thoughts, actions and beliefs in alignment

with the you who you wish you were?

That realization may not be easy to come by. It might take a lot of introspection.

Techniques like therapy, hypnosis and meditation are tools that can help you to access your meta-conscious mind. Culture offers a myriad of such tools.

My personal preferences lean to Self-Insight Meditation and EMDR therapy.

Eye movement desensitization and reprocessing (EMDR) is a psychotherapy developed by Francine Shapiro that emphasizes disturbing memories as the cause of psychopathology. I have found it invaluably heplful for me. Though it was developed specifically to heal from PTSD, it has also been very effective for people looking to "re-wire" their brains to achieve any number of goals: from quitting smoking to weight loss, to getting in touch with your Essential Self.

By alternately stimulating the left side of the brain, then the right side with either flashes of light, sound, or even tapping on meridian points, the idea is that the left and right brain become distracted.

The left and right brain are the places in the mind where emotion and rational thought are centered.

So, a talented psychotherapist, while performing EMDR techniques on a patient, will then ask the patient a series of skillful questions.

A classic, vague, example, just to illustrate the point: "How do you feel about that?" (And *that* can be anything.)

The left brain would rationalize and say something like, "It's just the way it has to be because it's how it's always been."

The right brain might say, "If feels safe, but terrifying!"

But neither of these are the True Answers.

By distracting the left and right hemispheres of the brain, EMDR allows the so-called Soul Center of the brain to step up and offer the Real Answer.

The Soul Center might say, "Well, it feels like that's been a behavior of mine since childhood. It began when I was nine because of certain specific circumstances. That behavior was very helpful at the time. But it seems as though that behavior is no longer serving me. I believe I should modify that behavior in the following, more useful way."

Now that's a half-page summary of EMDR therapy sessions which might take years to complete. But that's essentially the road-map to changing any behavior:

1. Recognize a conditioned response
2. Recognize where it came from
3. Realize it's no longer serving you,
4. Decide it's possible to change it
5. Identify what would be a more useful response
6. Manifest the change in your life

That's the gist of it!

Taking the action steps necessary to make a change is exponentially easier when the Soul Center of the mind steps up and realizes it's possible to change.

Here's the hard part: When you realize you are not who you want to be, and identify the action steps necessary to become who you want to be, the problem is, you may find that at least some (or in some cases, all) of the things, ideas and even people you previously anchored your identity to are going to fall away.

You may find yourself completely re-imagining your life and your identity because you've been living a life that's not consistent with the Real You.

This can be incredibly scary. That's a mid-life crisis.

> When You realize that the you You have been pretending to be is not the you You really are, that's a mid-life crisis. A mid-life solution is Re-creating yourself in Your own Image.

So who you think you are, who you have been acting like, the person other people see you as, might ... disappear ... completely.

So there's only one more question to ask:

Are you really ready for that?

A real Mid-Life Crisis does not begin by moving to a new home, changing careers or finding a new partner.

A real Mid-Life Crisis happens when you look in the mirror and find the Real You staring back, asking, "What on Earth are you doing. You are not who I am."

"You can get to where you want to be from wherever you are... but you must stop spending so much time noticing and talking about what you do not like about where you are."

—*Esther Hicks*

*"Freedom means you are unobstructed
in living your life as you choose.
Anything less is a form of slavery."*

*"Be miserable. Or motivate yourself.
Whatever has to be done,
it's always your choice."*

"Stop acting as if life is a rehearsal. Live this day as if it were your last. The past is over and gone. The future is not guaranteed."

"What we think determines what happens to us, so if we want to change our lives, we need to stretch our minds."

*"Go for it now.
The future is promised to no one."*

*"Transformation literally means
going beyond your form."*

*"What comes out of you when you are squeezed
is what is inside of you."*

—Wayne Dyer

Shining the Light of Conscious Awareness on the Invisible Walls of Unquestioned Assumptions

Realizing that you're ready for life to change, to invite new and amazing things into it that are in line with your deepest desires and in alignment with your dreams, is not something that happens overnight. It's a process. Learn to be patient with yourself.

There are a lot of pre-existing patterns in your mind that are going to crop up as soon as you shine the light of Conscious Awareness onto them.

What is the Light of Conscious Awareness?

The light of Conscious Awareness is the ability to identify, consciously, all the walls that have been subconsciously created in the past which keep you vibrating in the same patterns over and over and over again.

These walls are not made of brick or stone.

If they were, they would probably be easier to knock down.

Rather, I see them more like walls of crystal, beautiful geometric, yet transparent walls, keeping you from walking forward. These crystal walls obscure your vision of what is beyond them, yet at the same time, appear invisible to the Naked Mind.

When you take the Spotlight of Conscious Awareness out of your meta-conscious pocket, and shine the light onto the walls, their crystalline structure refracts the light back like a prism. And this reveals their existence in your mind for the first time.

When I first started identifying these walls locking in my own patterns of behavior, the first thing I realized is these walls were largely invisible. They are the unquestioned assumptions we make about how we're "supposed" to live. They have been built over years or decades of reinforcement, constructed so slowly and in the background of your mind, that you never noticed them going up. It's as if they've always been there. And since they are invisible and so pervasive, we tend to think of them as our identity.

But sometimes in our lives, the topography changes, and suddenly the vaguest scintilla of light illuminates these walls, revealing their location.

Imagine talking a stroll through the landscape of your sub-conscious mind. Imagine a large green field of gently rolling hills, extending to the horizon. There's a clear blue sky overhead, a beautiful puffy cloud or two, and, on the horizon, an enchanting pine forest, like something out of a fairy tale.

We'll call this the Forest of your Deepest Dreams. And within is contained a secret glade, a magical clearing. At the center of this clearing is a big beautiful diamond, the size of a boulder, and lodged within this diamond is the Sword of Truth.

The goal of our lives is to find our way into the Forest of our Deepest Dreams, find the path that leads to the clearing, and remove the Sword of Truth from the Diamond, and Manifest the Life of Your Dreams.

But for now we're standing on the hilltop in a prairie, merely conceptualizing the possibility of the forest and the clearing at its center, afraid to even dream about the diamond and the sword.

Yet we feel, sub-consciously, a profound sense that we must explore the forest.

So we look toward the trees, obscured though they are behind our crystal walls. Yet evidence of them seeps into our mind: we can smell their verdant sap as the first light of dawn comes over the horizon, touches the treetops, warming the air, and enticing the pines to release their soft, gentle scent into the morning air.

"Ah, a lovely pine forest!," your mind says to itself,

standing on a hilltop, "Smells enchantingly magical. That's where I want to spend the rest of my days. I can even imagine the wonderful soft needles beneath my feet as I walk through the trees! Ok, self, let's go!"

With enthusiastic effort and joy, you begin trotting, jogging, skipping and dancing towards the forest.

But before you get too far, "Oooowwww! Damn, that hurt!"

You've just collided, at a headlong gallop, nose first, into an invisible wall, blocking your way toward the forest.

You look around, and see no barriers. You walk ahead again.

Sure enough, thwunk!, you run into the wall again as you step forward.

And there's no way around this invisible barrier.

You can't even see it.

But you can feel it, keeping you from your destination.

So now you withdraw from your pocket a powerful flashlight, turn it on, shine it into the air, and sure enough!, the light it casts reveals before you the existence of a previously invisible wall.

This is the flashlight of Conscious Awareness.

Now you can see the wall.

You can see what it's made of.

See its texture.

See some cracks beginning to form.

Now the hard work begins.

"Now, self, why in the world did you ever erect an invisible crystal wall here, right in the middle of this pristine prairie, blocking the path into the forest?

And the self in reply says, "That's not for you to know. Just trust me, it's important. Stay where you are. Do not pass go. Do not collect $200."

In this case there needs to be a certain amount of healthy rejection of self-authority.

In which case you say, "Screw you, self! This wall is absurd. I'm not going to stay where you tell me! I'm going into the forest. Who gave you the right to tell me what to do, anyway?"

"Who gave *me* the right? I'm Yourself. What gives *you* the right to think you know better than *me?*"

And thus commences the battle of wits between the You who You think You are (the Identity you've constructed and tied to your Personality), and the Essential Self who you really are.

So, Personality Self, meet Essential Self.

The Essential Self is that part of you that dreams deep passionate dreams and knows beyond the shadow of all walls that you absolutely can manifest any dream that you can dream, create any reality you can imagine.

And the only thing standing in your way is the illusion of self-identity you've been protecting by erecting crystal walls, proclaiming, "Thou shalt not pass!"

Good thing the Essential Self carries the Light of Conscious Awareness.

For we'll find, that as soon as we shine the flashlight onto those walls, they begin, slowly to simply dissolve.

Before the light of Conscious Awareness shines forth, your mind is a prisoner of its own unquestioned assumptions.

But as soon as we begin to question those previously unquestioned assumptions, we can then begin to ask:

What is the root of these assumptions?

Where did they arise from?

Do they still serve me?

So, then, we should try as much as possible to keep training our mind to be consciously aware of what is subconsciously controlling our thoughts, feelings, and reactions to stimuli by shining the flashlight of Conscious Awareness onto all of our unquestioned assumptions.

We can begin cultivating this awareness by asking ourselves, "Why am I behaving the way I am?"

And be open to whatever the answer is, with no thought of judgment or emotional response to the underlying current of sub-conscious waves controlling the torrent of emotions that arise.

The trick is to be aware of the sub-conscious current of thoughts, simply acknowledge it, and say, "Yeah, that's interesting, if no longer helpful."

Then in that space of complete self-acceptance, you can begin to ask yourself, "Self, now, is this underlying feeling still serving us? Or is it an outdated response given birth to by a notion in the past? Is this notion still applicable in the present?"

If the answer is no, then we can begin to gently give ourself permission to no longer respond in the way we have been.

We can become aware of how our existing responses are not tied to our identity. This is a common thought pattern. We think that our responses make us who we are, and without them, we wouldn't have a sense of identity and we would be lost.

But our true identity in fact is buried beneath layers and layers of sub-conscious undercurrents, only to be found beyond the barrier of the invisible walls we have erected in the middle of a pristine prairie that we run into when trying to reach the Forest of our Deepest Dreams.

Those currents oftentimes dominate our lives, the walls constrict us, confine us to very small space in which we allow ourselves the freedom to roam.

Those walls give us a very constricted and false sense of identity, and security, which we cling to. And it's the attachment to the false identity of ourselves which keeps us from transcending our patterns of behavior—keeps us from realizing that those patterns are not actually us, but something keeping the real us from shining forth.

The quest therefore is to find the true Path of Your-Soul, which leads down through the rolling hills into the Forest of Your Deepest Dreams, where, ultimately we Quest to remove the Sword of Truth from its Diamond, and manifest the life of our dreams.

*"Enlightenment has nothing to do with
becoming better or being happier.
Enlightenment is the crumbling
away of untruth.
It's seeing through the facade of pretence.
It's the complete eradication of everything
we imagined to be true."*

*"The more you awaken, the more you feel, 'I might
not want to repeat the past, but I wouldn't have
one second of it any other way.'"*

*"This teaching is not so much a raft to carry you
to enlightenment as it is a fire to ignite the raft
you are now holding on to."*

*"Be a true representative of the goodness in
your heart, and don't expect it to be easy
or even noticed."*

*"Enlightenment means waking up to what you
truly are and then being that."*

*"Truth has no finality to it. It is not something
to be held on to. Truth is discovered minute to
minute or not at all."*

—*Adyashanti*

The Flashlight of Conscious Awareness

Our beliefs, expectations and ways of looking at the universe are the primary means by which reality manifests itself. Our consciousness creates the reality we experience.

And in the exact same way, our sub-conscious expectations—which arise from the aggregate of our previous experiences—can stand in our way, and back us into a corner where we think, "Since this is the only way I've ever experienced life, that means this is the only way it can be experienced." Rubbish! Hogwash!! That's a self-fulfilling prophecy! In that context, your ideas and preconceptions have created the exact reality that you think is the only possible one.

There is proof of this basic precept everywhere we

look. From the stereotype of people always falling into the same bad relationships over and over again, to the idea that 'the apple doesn't fall too far from the tree,' and so on.

All of which is actually a very empowering way to look at the world, if we simply tweaked our perception of things just a hair. Instead of saying: 'I'm trapped in these patterns,' you can instead look at that as compelling evidence that the patterns you create are actually the very vibrations that bring about whatever it is that happens in your life.

Next comes the real trick! *Shine the flashlight of awareness onto those patterns until they glow in the darkness of your sub-conscious mind and become visible to the meta-conscious mind.* And once you see them, they become undeniable.

And once recognized, it becomes possible to create different patterns and change your reality.

Our thoughts, the way we conceive the world, is precisely what creates reality.

You get to choose: what do you want that reality to look like?

Terraforming the Egoic Landscape

In Science Fiction, there is the theoretical concept of taking an existing planet, a moon, or other dead form, and modifying it to be Earth-like, complete with an atmosphere, liquid water, and all other components necessary to the existence of human life. That is, taking a non-Earth like planet and making it Earth-like so that human life can colonize it.

What Western Culture does to individuals is much the same. When we are born, we are a blank slate, a clean canvas. Through years and years of living and abiding within the socially conditioned cultural framework, our minds become "terraformed" into personalities which manifest in a way which makes them compatible with the existing cultural landscape.

Western Civilization has a very rigid and narrow notion of which behavioral traits are allowable, which are taboo, and which types of things are acceptable for one to do in one's life.

In short, all of our personalities, our egos, have been terraformed into ones that can fit nicely into the narrow mold that society has carved out for us.

Most of these behaviors are relatively arbitrary. The culturally-conditioned behaviors that are allowable, at their core, really have very little (or nothing at all) to do with what behaviors are going to allow us to live happy, fulfilling, purpose-driven lives. The allowable behaviors are really only created to allow individuals to best fit as a cog into the wheel of society, to be worker bees in a dysfunctional hive that is really not conducive to individuality.

In *Star Trek,* there is the adage that "The needs of the many outweigh the needs of the few, or the one."

This adage, presented by the highly logical Vulcan race, is quite profoundly true. However, the thing that the hive mind of individuals must constantly question is, "Are the needs of the many truly being served by the culture we have created?"

The best definition of corruption and greed is, "The manipulation or exploitation of the needs of the many to serve the needs of the few, or the one."

And this is precisely the sickness that has infected our civilization like a plague.

And it is precisely this motivation which forms the foundation for the untruths we have been told about who we each are. We have tied our identities to those false beliefs for as many years as we have been alive so that the process of unravelling the onion of identity can be terrifying and overwhelming.

But it appears with each passing day, that there are more and more of us willing to take the plunge and ask the real question: Who am I, really?

> If you've been starting to ask yourself this Big Question, too, take heart: you are not alone!

It is up to each one of us to re-evaluate the narrative we were told, hold it up to the light of Conscious Awareness and as the question, "Is my life serving the needs of the many? Or am I merely conforming to the narrative society has woven and being manipulated into serving the very, very few at the top of an ever-destabilizing pyramid?"

The Guardians of our Culture (without putting a face to any specific '*them*'), is the very powerful force that keeps individuals locked into a wheel of action that serves only the Highest Good of the Few.

But society itself at this point in its evolution does not appear to be serving the needs of the Many, or the All. It is merely serving itself so that its own cogs keep on spinning in place. This is a hamster wheel we need to get off.

It's up to each of us to question all of the assumptions we have taken as Cultural Gospel, and ask, "Is this the life I was put on this world to live? And if not, then what life was I actually put here to live?"

> *"Get Busy Living, or Get Busy Dying."*
> *—The Shawshank Redemption*

And that can be an incredibly scary question. The answer involves no less than unraveling everything you have ever been told and finding your own true identity buried under the mask of everything society has told you to be true.

Question all of your assumptions and believed truths.

Ask yourself, "Do the so-called truths I was told actually, deeply, feel true? Or do they feel like stories?"

We are not the stories we have been told. And the stories we have been told cover up the truth. That truth is buried beneath an avalanche that has been happening for thousands of years. It's time to dig ourselves out and into the Light of Truth.

We must un-bury ourselves so that we can find out who we each truly are, why we were put here, and what it was we were meant to accomplish with our lives.

When all of the untruths are exposed, we can finally begin to open ourselves up to asking the real question, "Why am I really here?"

Gateways into the Meta-Conscious

Psychoanalysis
Hypnotherapy
Self-hypnosis
Prayer
Meditation
EMDR
Emotional Freedom Technique (EFT)
Neuro-linguistic programming
Psychedelics

These are just some of the gateways into the subconscious mind that can be walked through consciously. Each technique works slightly differently, and some will be more effective for certain individuals than others. But the purpose of them all is similarly aligned: to give the conscious mind access to the sub-conscious patterns of behavior that are controlling our actions without our consent. Developing that awareness is the first tool in our toolbox necessary for change.

Standing on the other side of those gateways is necessarily to reveal our subconscious thought patterns. It is then up to us to question the validity of those thought patterns with our conscious mind, and then begin to re-wire those patterns which are no longer serving us with out meta-consciousness.

The meta-consciousness is an idea that has only just begun crop up in the cultural consciousness. It was only 100 years ago or so that Jung introduced us to the subconsciousness. The meta-consciousness is the part of your mind that has control over the sub-conscious thought patterns, and even over regular consciousness itself.

Practice Doesn't Make Perfect... Perfect Practice Makes Perfect

When we are practicing a new skill, from learning how to play a new sport, to practicing a musical instrument, there's a process which is both beneficial and potentially harmful.

While we are initially learning, our conscious mind is aware of every minute physical movement involved in performing the action. As we practice the same action over and over again, the information becomes ingrained in our mind, so that after awhile, we no longer have to consciously think about what we're doing. Muscle-memory takes over and the action moves into the realm of the subconscious mind.

In the example of learning to play a new song on a musical instrument, at first we have to be consciously attentive to every note, in sequence.

With the repetition of practice, the sequence becomes transcribed into the back of the mind, and we can then just "Flow" with the piece of music without thinking about it. That's when the real magic happens, when we're really in the zone and play fluidly.

But if we learn the piece incorrectly, then the incorrect notes become transcribed into the back of the mind.

So what happens when we realized we encoded an incorrect pattern into the back of our mind?

We then have the daunting task of un-learning the incorrect note before we can learn the correct one, and replace it in our sub-conscious mind.

It can then take at least 100 repetitions of playing the correct note in order to un-learn the incorrect note. In other words, un-learning is much harder than learning.

This is true not just with music, but with every pattern that is deeply ingrained in our minds.

And in order to un-learn, we have to engage the meta-conscious mind.

Living from the Meta-Consciouness

Learning how to live from a place of meta-consciousness is an essential skill to develop when choosing to live a life of Conscious Intention and skillfully navigating the power of intention.

Regular consciousness itself does not have this power. Only the meta-consciousness does.

Operating from a place of meta-conscious awareness, humans (and possibly all living organisms) have the power to heal themselves of all traumas or dis-eases within the body and mind.

From afflictions of the mind such as anxiety and depression and PTSD, to dis-eases manifested in the body, such as Cancer and HIV, the power of the meta-consciousness can heal these from a place of energetic awareness and on a physical-cellular level.

There is evidence that even Western medicine has identified that the power of prayer remarkably increases the healing capacity of the human body. Prayer affects consciousness, and consciousness affects reality.

Dr. Max Gersen showed almost a century ago (c. 1920s) that Cancer will go into complete remission with proper diet. Western Medicine doesn't stand behind his results, and banned him from practicing his Healing Arts in America. The American Cancer Association has tremendous pull, and is, in fact, the single most profitable non-profit organization in the world.

Gersen was effectively exiled from America, and set up his clinic in Mexico, where to this day, his family continues to carry on his work and is curing cancer in people willing to take the leap of faith and put Western

Medicinal cures second in favor of healthy diet.

For the reader interested in more information on Max Gersen, there are numerous documentaries available on Netflix or Amazon Prime that discuss the specifics of his treatment.

But it's much more than healthy diet which is curing cancer in Mexico at the Gersen Institute. It's the Power of Meta-Conscious intention that truly makes the difference.

Meta-conscious intention is a power all humans can develop. It's also something most of us know too little about.

But as we learn more and more about this reality, I have no doubt that we will begin witnessing a worldwide phenomenon of seemingly spontaneous healing occurring in humans that Western Medicine has identified as "incurable (by Western Medicine)."

> Everyone has the ability to access the meta-conscious mind, and heal themselves.

The Healing Arts are just one tangible way the Power of Meta-Conscious Intention manifests. I believe that people diagnosed with terminal illnesses provide a good case study for the existence of this power. In fact, a diagnosis such as that can jump-start the mind into turning on the power of Conscious Intention.

But a diagnosis of a terminal illness is by no means necessary to gain access to this latent human ability.

It exists in all of us, at all times, just beneath the surface (or above the surface, as the case may be), and whenever we decide to tap into it, we learn it's been there, all the while.

The gateway into unleashing this power comes in the form of various techniques that unlock the door, such as hypnosis, meditation, and psychoanalysis (if practiced correctly by a true Healer.) Not every practitioner with a PhD is a True Healer, and in fact the most powerful healers I have come across in my lifetime have no credentials and make no claims whatsoever. Nevertheless, as soon as one has a conversation with a True Healer, it becomes immediately obvious who they Are and what their mindset has allowed them to manifest in their own lives. Have you ever met anyone like this?

A far greater number of us have the latent ability to be healers than is generally known. Everyone has the ability to access the meta-conscious mind, and heal themselves. And when the true path of healing is undertaken, showing others the existence of this path gives them the ability to walk it, too. So every human on the planet has the power to be a healer, merely through leading by example.

And this is a key component of the healing that is taking place on this planet right now. This is a pivotal time in human history. We are finally, for the first time, Awakening to the idea that Consciousness creates Reality.

To allow this power to truly gain a foothold on our civilization, we need to achieve critical mass (The Hundredth Monkey Effect), where the vast majority of people come into contact with this idea and begin living in accordance with it.

Techniques such as hypnosis, meditation and psychoanalysis are just some of the most widely accepted techniques which enable this change to occur. There are others, currently taboo in the context of our civilization. Specifically, these are plant-based spiritual medicines, starting with Marijuana and including all of the more powerful, natural plant-based, consciousness-altering herbs, such as Ayahuasca.

We must ask ourselves, "Why does the subconscious mind of our civilization consider natural plant-based, consciousness-altering herbs, taboo, and even illegal?"

> The feeling of paranoia some marijuana smokers claim to feel? That's not actually paranoia. That's the sub-conscious mind revealing to consciousness how it's really, truly feeling deep down.

My personal experiences with some of these herbs reveal, with no question in my mind, that these substances are one very powerful shortcut into the meta-conscious mind. They are by no means necessary to crossing that threshold, but given how tightly locked that door is kept by the Gatekeepers of our Civilization, these herbal supplements can be, if used responsibly and with Intention, the very thing some people need to break the lock on the gateway of the meta-conscious mind and start living life with the Intention necessary to break their pre-existing patterns and take a quantum leap ahead in the evolution of their own consciousness.

For anyone considering plant-based medicines as a tool to help them on their path of raising their consciousness, I highly recommend doing quite a bit of self-work first, to really get at the core of their own personality before being thrust too quickly into a realm that will be utterly and completely terrifying and un-welcoming to a Stranger in a Strange Land.

What do I mean by that?

One example: The feeling of paranoia some marijuana smokers claim to feel. That's not actually paranoia. That's them becoming aware for the first time of the things they're really, truly feeling deep down inside.

Those types of sensations are the sub-conscious mind revealing itself. And the effect is even much more pronounced on stronger plant-based medicines. For people not ready for that type of experience, that's going to result in one Bad Trip.

That's not the place to begin the journey.

I truly believe that a powerful first step is the simple act of sitting quietly with your own thoughts in meditation.

Look for a Buddhist Temple in your area, or simply sit at home, silently and by yourself for 20 minutes. There's nothing more to it than that.

Meditation & Hypnosis

Self-Insight Meditation is one technique I found most effective for me in my own life, which is why it's

something I'm so passionate about teaching others now.
Stop.
Sit.
Listen to your own thoughts.
This can be done in a group, or simply on your own in silence.

Just turn off the TV and sit there. And do nothing. Just be alone with yourself.

Nothing could be easier in the whole world.
Or harder.
But that really is the first step in developing a meditation practice.

Meditation is a form of self-hypnosis.

When meditating, listening to hypnosis tapes or going to a hypnotherapist, along with other techniques for accessing the meta-consciousness, the mind's brain waves move from a state of Beta Waves to Theta Waves.

During the Theta Wave state, the brain becomes up to 100 times more capable of re-wiring itself. Theta Waves are what meditation and hypnosis encourages, and is associated with my definition of the meta-conscious mind.

The 5 Brain States

1. Gamma State: (30 — 100Hz) This is a state of hyperactivity. If over stimulated, it can lead to anxiety. This state of mind is associated with the fight-or-flight response.

2. Beta State: (13 — 30Hz) This is where we function for most of the day in our so-called "productive" culture.

This is a state of the "working" or "thinking mind": analytical, planning, assessing, obsessing, and categorizing.

3. Alpha State: (9 — 13Hz) Associated with feelings or calmness. Can be achieved during a yoga class, a walk in the woods, a pleasurable sexual encounter, or any activity that helps relax the body and mind.

4. Theta State: (4 — 8Hz) We're able to begin meditation. This is the point where the verbal/thinking mind transitions to the meditative/visual mind. We begin to move from the planning mind to a deeper state of awareness, with stronger intuition, more capacity for wholeness and self-awareness.

5. Delta State: (1—3 Hz) Tibetan monks who have been meditating for decades can reach this in an alert, awakened phase.

Insight is 20/20

How many times have you heard the expression, "Hindsight is 20/20"?

We usually invoke it when talking about something we regret.

Then we might say to ourselves, "At least I know better for next time."

Think about it. How many times have you said that?

But more importantly, how many times do we actually learn the lesson our mistakes were trying to teach us?

Hindsight is thinking about the past. But that's not all that useful on its own. Hindsight only works in partnership with its significant other: insight.

One way of thinking about insight is that it's learning how to see the patterns between the past and the present, before it's too late.

Invoke insight at the first moment you notice an old pattern that's repeating.

Right now, at this very moment, is when insight is needed the most: use it to connect a past event (which we told ourselves we could learn from) with a present event, happening now. Recognize the recurring pattern at the moment it starts to repeat: that's insight.

Insight is recognizing in this moment, that this is one of those times.

Then, only then, by seeing that, can you cultivate the mindfulness, intent, compassion and action necessary for changing your behavior, and acting in a different, skillful, insightful way.

We can only learn how to do this through hindsight and insight, together. It's not enough to just take time to reflect on the past. We also need to practice insight, which is necessary for noticing when the pattern is starting to happen again. And noticing it in time to break the cycle.

A Continuous Now, Instead of Clock Time

In order to allow hindsight and insight to work most effectively together, we have to use a better definition of "The Now" than what is generally accepted.

Culturally, we are told that The Now is now, now, now, now, now, forever ticking past like the second hand on a clock. But this is not the now. This is just clock time.

A more useful concept of The Now is the continuous

string of past, present and future moments that are linked together to reveal a pattern.

So let's consider an example: imagine a friend or a lover, someone who is important to you in your life. Imagine spending time with them, in whatever way you enjoy. Imagine snuggling on a couch, or eye-gazing with that person, or just having lunch.

The Now you are experiencing with them at this very moment is not just the activity of snuggling on the couch, but rather is all the moments you have spent with them in the past, leading up to the present. That is The Now. It's the pattern that you create when you're together.

> The Now is a continuous string of past, present and future moments that consciousness links together to create a pattern.

Or in the case of reading this book. Clock time says you're reading this word Now, then this word, Now, then the next word, Now.

But individual words have no context when read in isolation, so how can reading each word constitute a Now? It doesn't. The Now of reading this book is the time you spent reading it last night, the time tonight that you are reading this book, and the time when you will read it again tomorrow, or next week. This pattern, this accumulation of similar experiences, coalesces into a continuous now.

Everyone of us is living in a multiplicity of continuous nows. And that's a much more useful way to think about the way we are navigating through time.

The words you will read tomorrow will give you a deeper insight into the words you read today, and those you read yesterday.

What we generally think of as the past, present and future are actually all different aspects in the same continuous Now. They inform each other, and only together, do they reveal the deeper meaning, the deeper pattern, of what the Now actually is, in the way you are experiencing it in this moment.

In this way, hindsight and insight work together.

And when they cooperate in this way, we can use the power of hindsight and insight together to more insightfully imagine how the next instance of the now might manifest, and make the most of it.

Looked at another way, what we generally think of as the past and future are not the separate things we imagine them to be.

Imagine the past as the ocean, and the future as the sky. In this analogy, the Now is merely the imaginary horizon that appears where the past and future merge, where each seemingly disappears into the other.

The now is the horizon of your life.

And if you are deeply insightful about the past and the present moment together, it becomes possible to achieve what almost may appear to be a sense of clairvoyance about the future. You can see the clouds in the sky reflected in the ripples on the ocean surface.

You can intuit the existence of the future by deeply

understanding the lessons and meaning of the past. The Now is therefore an ongoing continuum, not events that are isolated in time from one another.

This use of insight allows for a far greater degree of understanding meaning in your life and how all the seemingly different events in it go together to create a unified whole.

In a larger context, your entire life is merely one continuous now.

Through the power of insight, we can manifest and intuit what that life means and what is likely to happen next, so that we can be best prepared and bring the best part of ourselves into each moment as it presents itself. The imaginary vanishing point on the horizon is ever-changing.

And just as the world's first sailors learned how to navigate the oceans by looking at the stars, we can learn the lessons of the past and future by understanding that these two concepts are really two sides of the same coin.

The present is reflected in the past and future, simultaneously.

Your Personal Path of Least Resistance

At first thought, 'living a life of intention' and 'just going with the flow' can seem like paradoxical statements. Doesn't 'just go with the flow' imply a lack of conscious intention?

The true path of least resistance is always going with your personal Tao. But the first step in aligning with your personal Tao requires intention and insight meditation … and learning how to be completely open and honest with your Essential Self is crucial.

Really going with the flow first implies that you have come to consciously understand where your own personal Tao wants to take you, and to stop standing in your own way. So many of the things we do in life are actually just ways that we keep ourselves from moving forward. This is the 'personal contradictory principle' which is when we say "Yes!" because we think we want something, but we really don't. Or we say, "No!" when we're too scared to admit that we really do want whatever it is.

And what's the reason we have our wires crossed so much of the time? We don't really know ourselves. Or more often, we really are literally 'scared to death' of being completely honest with ourselves.

Scared to death? Yes. Death of the personality, of the ego, which is the mask we hide behind, and that's what stands in the way of the Essential Self finding self-expression.

Taking a "vacation from yourself," where you step back from your life and experience something radically different, can be a radically effective way to see yourself from a seemingly external point of view. This allows the walls of egoic perception to begin to erode, so that, once back within the confines of your "real life," you can begin the much harder task of experiencing the same things in different ways. This separation is one very helpful, arguably essential, step for transcending the sensation of feeling "stuck."

When we can learn to see our own life from a less-subjective perspective, we can glimpse how the patterns that have been manifesting in our life create the life we're living. And when learn to see that, the awareness arises that we create our own reality through our thoughts and actions.

The "Power of Intention," in the popular parlance of

our time, is a vague understanding of a very fundamental principle, for which a better term might be, "The Power of Meta-Conscious Awareness."

That which we are aware of, what we focus on, is precisely what we find and attract into our lives.

Australian Aborigines have the ability to find water in the seemingly vapid desert during a walkabout. It's not that they "intend" the water to be there. They are simply keenly in tune with where the water is and, in this way, they're able to find it. The same is true of anything in life that anyone focuses on.

> What is the True Path of YourSoul, that which your destiny is aligned with Manifesting?

In a universe of infinite possibilities, where anything that can happen does happen, and also where time is non-linear, those two assumptions together imply that everything that we focus on becomes manifest. Consciousness is the primary unity of the universe.

Consciousness creates reality.

And, moreover, conscious blockages, like the illusion of our personalities and our phobias, fears and desires, simply block things from manifesting.

We can transcend all our blockages, get out of our own way, and create, through conscious attention, awareness, mindfulness and focus, the precise reality our soul's true destiny is aligned with.

Be careful what you wish for. You will get it, if you focus on it. You will.

The deeper, harder question, is: What is the True Path of YourSoul, that which you're destiny is aligned with Manifesting?

Focus on that reality, and it will Manifest, and that is the true gateway to achieving unconditional happiness, which is found at the intersection of fulfillment and purpose.

> *"At the center of your being you have the answer, you know who you are and know what you want."*
>
> —*Lao Tzu*

> *"Life is a series of natural and spontaneous changes. Don't resist them—that only creates sorrow. Let reality be reality. Let things flow naturally forward in whatever way they like."*
>
> —*Lao Tzu*

20/20 Consciousness

Generally speaking, most of us make out very little detail about what we're aware of in our lives. We focus on things that don't matter, like having money, while having only a fuzzy notion about what's really important, such as cultivating our passions, and what it means to live a purposeful, meaningful, life.

As such, we have only a fuzzy awareness of other people, how to be a great artist, how to be a good friend or a great lover. We simply haven't learned how to focus on these things, because we haven't realized they are truly, deeply important and meaningful.

We don't really realize that focusing on what's important to us is what's really going to make us happy. We have a very vague awareness of the threads of life all around us, which weave the tapestry of our lives, and which we ourselves are weaving.

Buddhism identifies consciousness as the sixth sense. And there's nothing metaphysical about it. Buddhism simply proposes that, exactly like sight, smell, touch, scent and sound, consciousness is a very real way in which our physical being becomes aware of the Universe around us.

And just how everyone's eyesight and hearing can be better or worse, so, too, can consciousness.

When we have less than 20/20 vision, we can correct with contacts or eyeglasses. Hearing with hearing-aids.

Consciousness with Meditation.

So what would it feel like to have 20/20 consciousness?

Imagine standing at the end of a field and looking at an Oak Tree in the distance. Imagine you have never seen an Oak Tree up close, that you have terrible eyesight and have never worn glasses. What would that Oak Tree look like to you?

It would appear merely to be a brown trunk rising into an oval green halo.

Now, since you have never seen an Oak Tree up close, you would have no concept that the green halo you perceive is actually a collection of individual leaves.

Now, walk across the field toward the Oak Tree. Imagine you have perfect eyesight up close, you just can't see far away. Suddenly, as you approach the tree, all the leaves come into focus!

So, what does this have to do with consciousness?

In this analogy, standing at the far end of the field

and looking at the vague image of an Oak Tree but not seeing the leaves is analogous to not being able to see the minute patterns in your life and how those patterns go together to form the tapestry of life you're weaving.

Looked at another way, the far end of the field where the Oak Tree is can be thought of as the future, and you're a great distance away, standing in the present.

20/20 consciousness would allow you to make out the leaves of the Oak Tree from the far end of the field, and see details about the Life of Your Dreams standing back at a much greater distance.

20/20 consciousness also makes the path leading towards the Oak Tree much easier to navigate. With bad eyesight, you might get caught up in some barbed wire as you walk through the field, or even step on a land-mine!

20/20 consciousness allows you to see the path of least resistance much more clearly as you walk towards your future. It also allows you to envision that future to a much greater level of detail.

Meditation is like Lasik surgery for your consciousness.

Only it's not a quick-fix. It takes a daily practice and lots of hard work.

Buddhism calls Meditation the practice of developing minute mindfulness.

So this, then, is how Self-Insight Meditation works:
Ask yourself what's important to you, and pay attention to the answer without judgment, an emotional response or bias. Simply notice the answer and say,

"That's interesting." Then, learn how to think about the way you're thinking about things. For example, why don't you devote more time to doing art if you know it's important to you?

Ask yourself and pay attention to the answer. Then ask yourself if that makes sense and if you want to continue living that way.

> *"I am an artist at living,*
> *my work of art is my life."*
> —*D.T. Suzuki*

Your life is a work of art. Paint it with every brush stroke, like a master creating a masterpiece. You only get one canvas. Paint with intention. Know that every brush stroke you make which was a mistake is going to take a lot more effort later to smudge out. What this means is: *don't make your entire life a learning opportunity. Insight is better than hindsight.*

Live your life with intention, and be aware of what's important to you, and focus on that with 20/20 minute mindfulness.

Don't allow your entire life to be merely
a learning opportunity.
Insight is better than hindsight.
Learn the lesson, then apply the change.

At first, it's best to avoid deep inner-personal problems as the focus of Self-Insight Meditation.

Start with simple tasks, such as: Why do I drink 5 cups of coffee in the morning?

Cultivate acute awareness the next time you ask yourself that question. Be aware of yourself trying to help yourself. Focus on that, not vaguely, but in sharp, detailed focus, 20/20 vision, like you're looking at a vast mural in an art gallery of yourself and appreciating every brush stroke.

Because you are painting your life with every action you take and every thought you think.

"Meditation is Lasik surgery for your consciousness."

Water does not fear a Waterfall

*"If water, flowing down a peaceful river,
were to become aware that downstream
it was headed inexorably for a waterfall,
would it be frightened?"*

Water does not fear a waterfall. A consciousness observing nature would become aware that water flows faster and faster as it approaches the waterfall.

Now, we might think, "Oh, it's like the water is rushing to get there!" But it's not that at all. The water merely follows its natural course. It Flows in the only way it can, always towards the waterfall, never away.

When streams flow smoothly and no waterfall is up ahead, the water simply enjoys the flow. The more playful waters form whirlpools, as if dancing and enjoying the harmony.

If we became too aware of the path of the river of our lives, we would worry incessantly about the upcoming waterfall. But since the river of life is not straight, but, like all rivers, weaves a graceful S-shape through the topography, we are given only glimpses of the ultimate path, and can only be present to one bend at a time.

Powerfully present minds can learn to see bends in the river much further upstream than is generally thought. But powerful minds that learn to see without first being calm, clear and centered may not do well to have the knowledge of the path, for they will be overcome with fear and anxiety of what is coming up ten bends from now. Minds that are clear can know of the tenth bend, and simultaneously remain present to the one they are currently in, and focus attention here, doing nothing more to prepare for the tenth than merely being truly present in the moment. The advantage of being truly present in the moment allows us to practice being truly present for the tenth when it arrives. Thus, the harmony that a clear and focused mind has is that when the tenth comes, it does not become frightened or scared. Rather, these minds can fully enjoy the surprise and wondrous beauty of the tenth bend, not having the awareness of the surprise polluted by the fear-inducing feeling that it was unknown.

It was, in fact, known all along that the tenth was always coming. Just not consciously attended to until the time was right.

When awake and aware minds are fully prepared for

the surprise when it comes (by virtue of their being aware of it all along, co-creating it all along) these minds are most wondrously surprised when the glimpsed-at-vision manifests in so much more of a profoundly beautiful way than the thinking mind could possibly have conceived. And had the thinking mind grasped at a conception, that concept would have blinded the mind to the harmony there is in reality.

Japanese architecture employs arches, curves and bends, and avoids straight lines.

The first time I heard of this, I was told that this is so because the Japanese believe that evil spirits move in straight lines, which sounds superstitious.

Later, I learned the deeper Truth, told from the opposite viewpoint, which makes all the sense in the world without employing superstition at all.

All the good things that come to us in our lives take curvy paths, meandering, cyclical swirls, touching our consciousness like the beautiful S-shape of a river.

Nothing in nature moves in a straight line.

Meditation can help us become aware of all the thoughts in our heads that are swirling around constantly below the surface all the time. There are dozens of voices saying things all the time, commenting, criticizing and praising, being bothered and bothersome.

Each of these voices can be isolated and identified clearly, paid attention to, and each assigned useful and helpful tasks (threads to weave in their own unique way) and by thus working together with your own mind, in harmony on different things, a unified consciousness can effectively envision a wonderful reality and Manifest it.

BlindThought

There are more than two ways of doing anything. Have the courage to find your own way.

At first blush, that statement might seem mindlessly obvious, and a terrible sentence in a book that proposes to change the way you look at everything.

But think about it some more.

You might realize, intellectually, that there's more than one way of doing anything, but do you behave that way in real life?

One of my key suppositions is many of us too often act in a way inconsistent with our fundamental beliefs.

Frequently, we believe (intellectually) one thing, but behave in a way completely inconsistent with that belief (often in a way that supports the opposite belief), and we don't realize that our actions and beliefs stand in stark contradiction to each other.

This type of belief-behavior duality is one of the fundamental causes of unhappiness, discord and disharmony.

A good word for this phenomenon is "BlindThought."

It's a blind spot in the way we are thinking.

We don't realize that we're thinking and acting in contradictory ways.

This is one of the ways in which the expression "We're Asleep" is meant.

> Buddhism teaches that one way to an unconditional happy life is when thoughts, actions, behaviors and motivations all become perfectly aligned.

There are a couple of key aspects of BlindThought which can be transcended through meditation:

1) Too often, we don't realize what's true and what's simply been told to us as true. We don't always realize that we believe something simply because we've been told it's true.

2) We don't always realize where our motivations come from for doing the things we do. The motivations we think are our own are sometimes the motivations society has told us we should have. We parrot those back, and falsely internalize them as our own. But oftentimes, we're simply not self-aware (awake) enough to realize we're not being honest with ourselves.

Always have the courage to follow your True Beliefs, regardless of what others believe, and take the time necessary to truly identify your beliefs and why you believe them.

That is a real gateway to aligning with the true Path of YourSoul.

Always have the courage and take the time to ask yourself:

"Why do I believe what I believe?"

"Does this belief I think I believe align with my Essential Self?"

Have the courage to be a True Individual and believe what you believe because you believe it. It doesn't matter what anyone else thinks, so long as you think it through for yourself at a minute level of mindfulness.

> *"A paradox is a truth standing on its head to draw attention to itself."*
> *—Unknown*

> *"In any duality, both sides are true. Transcending duality is the same as transcending paradox: take the middle path, accepting that both sides are true, seen from opposite points of view."*

Self-Insight Meditation

So, now that we have discussed all the reasons why meditation might be helpful, it's time to look at the specific technique.

But, first, let's summarize.

We should meditate to know ourselves better because we want to live a life in line with our Essential Selves, not doing what we're told just because that's what we're told.

We want to lead better, happier, more fulfilling lives.

And the more and more of us who do this, the more culture changes away from its toxic mindset. Together, we can create a world that transcends the old paradigms that are no longer serving us, and become the Magical Civilzation we have the potential of becoming.

If we don't do this, we run the risk of Human Colony Collapse Disorder.

Remember: Change starts with You!

> "Be the Change
> You wish to see in the world."
> —Mahatma Gandhi

Self-Insight Meditation combines the spiritual teachings of Buddhism and Taoism with the classical Greek adage, "Know Thyself," which teaches that knowing who you are is the true path to wisdom, happiness and a fulfilling life.

Self-Insight Meditation encourages us to spend time reflecting (meditating) on our true selves and inner desires. It can help us find the true Path of YourSoul, which leads to achieving the life of our dreams.

This is the primary technique I teach in my Higher Self Ascension Workshops.

Talk to 10 different people about meditation, and you'll get 10 different definitions for what meditation is.

It can be spiritual, but doesn't have to be.
It can be Buddhist-y or Transcendental or Seek.
But it doesn't have to be.

Definition of Meditation from Wikipedia:

"The word meditation has a multitude of meanings. Meditation has been practiced since antiquity as a component of numerous religious traditions and beliefs. Meditation often involves an internal effort to self-regulate the mind

in some way. Meditation is often used to clear the mind and ease many health concerns, such as high blood pressure, depression, and anxiety. It may be done sitting, or in an active way.

Meditation may involve generating an emotional state for the purpose of analyzing that state, or cultivating a particular mental response to various phenomena, such as compassion. The term "meditation" can refer to the state itself, as well as to practices or techniques employed to cultivate the state.

In Buddhist practice, meditation is generally regarded as letting go of all thoughts and conceptions."

Instead of letting thoughts pass by, as in the Buddhist tradition, Self-Insight Meditation is a little different.

Self-Insight Meditation proposes that we should know ourselves, and take the time to know ourselves well. Knowing why we are doing what we're doing, questioning our motivations, and knowing the difference between our personality and our Essential Self. When we learn that there's a difference, we can recognize that sometimes our personality is doing things that our essential self would never agree to! But we don't know we're doing it! That's why we continue to do it. And that's one of the key causes unhappiness, depression, and feelings of unhappiness.

Self-Insight Meditation is a technique that asks specific questions about why we're doing what we're doing, and if we really want to be doing that.

So, do you?

And if not, we can't just say, "Ok, now, self! Stop doing that!"

We have to be gentle with ourselves, using positive affirmations like, "Now, self, I understand why you're doing that, and it's served us well in the past. I believe it's no longer as useful as it once was. Would you be wiling to try this other (specific) thing instead?"

Trying to get ourselves to listen to reason can be really hard!

Self-Insight Meditation can help us recognize and identify specific patterns of behavior in our lives. We can then begin to see which ones are beneficial, and which ones may be detrimental to the life we want.

Self-Insight Meditation is a technique which allows us to recognize when our thoughts and actions are mis-aligned.

This can be done alone or in a group. Meditating in a group has a unique energy. It's very different from meditating alone. There is a resonance that accumulates when a community comes together with a like-minded intention.

So, to begin:

Introduction to Self-Insight

Identify a problem in your life.
Ask yourself this series of questions:
Why do I act this way?
What is the reason I behave this way?
What's my motivation for behaving this way?
Is this behavioral pattern actually the way I want to

be acting in this situation?

Can I imagine a different, more useful pattern of behavior that I can apply in this situation?

Does this pattern of behavior manifest in other areas of my life, and cause similar types of problems?

Rehearse the situation in your mind, and see how it could play out differently if you changed your behavior when it comes up the next time.

Ask yourself this next series of questions:

If I responded differently the next time this situation occurs, how would that change the outcome?

List specific details in your re-imagining

Identify particular parts of your life that don't feel like they're being lived in line with your Essential Self.

Are there ways that I'm living my life that don't feel like I'm being honest with myself?

What parts about myself am I hiding from myself?

Are there things I'd rather be doing than what I'm actually doing today?

What is stopping me from actually doing the things I need to be doing in order to be following my bliss?

Are these "reasons" actually just "excuses"?

Start with small problems, issues and circumstances. Don't start with large things. You'll want to take small bites first in order to get used to the idea of changing things. Change has a habit of starting off slowly, and building, building, building, until it reaches a crescendo. At some point, changes will begin to happen very, very rapidly. But this doesn't start happening all at once. There's a period of very slow growth at the beginning of this process. It will build and accumulate and aggregate over time until you're deep in the Flow of change.

One of the ways the mind works is that conditioned patterns of behavior are relegated to the "back of the mind." These behavioral patterns are habituated, and unquestioned. You employ this part of your mind when situations arise over and over again, so your mind doesn't need to spend a lot of energy thinking about the correct response to each individual situation. It's a pretty efficient mechanism.

The problem results when the behavior patterns that we relegate to the back of our minds no longer serve us. Perhaps it served us at one point in the past, but we can see how the techniques (or even defense mechanisms) we employed in the past can cause us harm later in life.

So we need to question that back-minded behavior, shine the spotlight of Conscious Awareness onto it, bring it to the light of day and question it: is this behavior really working? What would work better? Answer that question and start living in that way.

This is hard at first because now you're starting to live in the front of your mind, and that takes more work, more energy, more conscious attention. But don't worry! The goal is to un-do the old programming through conscious awareness, and replace those old patterns with new patterns.

Test out new patterns. If you find the new patterns are serving your highest good, your highest self, then at some point, they, too, could become relegated to the back part of your mind and, once there, they fully and completely replace the old, out-dated programs that were running.

Relegating new patterns to the back of the mind isn't entirely the goal, though, because it might cause more problems to crop up again later in life.

The goal is more in line with this notion:

Through employing this technique of questioning, over and over and over again, to a multiplicity of situations in your life, then this behavior itself begins to go into the back of your mind and you can begin to question every action, every behavior, and then, the act of questioning yourself, looking inward, that behavior itself becomes second nature.

When every experience you have in your life is held up to the spotlight of Conscious Awareness, then every event in your life becomes an opportunity for learning, an opportunity for asking: Did I handle that situation in a way that aligns with my Essential Self? Was that response the one that brought about the highest good? Can I refine that behavior even further the next time this situation comes up?

We can quest to always be constantly refining and re-defining our patterns of behavior so that every time, in every situation, we act not according to any old patterns, not in accord with any pre-programmed responses, but use each experience as a learning opportunity to understand what each particular situation itself asks for.

Learn how to gracefully navigate each and every situation that arises from a place of the Highest Self, of love, of bringing out the most good at all possible times and in all possible ways.

This act of living your life in such a way as to always be questioning the very core, getting to the very essence of every single event so that it can be deeply understood, and the most loving, useful action applied to each and every unique situation even has a term that you might be familiar with: this is a key component of Zen, by any other name.

*Nan-in, a Japanese master, served tea.
He poured his visitor's cup full,
and then kept on pouring.*

*The visitor watched the overflow until he no
longer could restrain himself.
"It is overfull. No more will go in!"*

*"Like this cup," Nan-in said, "you are full of
your own opinions and speculations.
How can I show you Zen
unless you first empty your cup?"*

—*Zen Koan*

Higher Self Ascension

Self-Insight Meditation is the technique I have been practicing my whole life. In 2015, when I realized I had completed the curriculum of Self Awareness I had set out for myself, my Higher Self called me to begin teaching this technique to others. The mediation circle meets once or twice a week, and Higher Self Ascension workshops are weekend retreats for the more advanced meditators.

However, having a personal, daily meditation practice is best. An effective technique is to meditate early in the morning, even the first thing upon Awakening, so that it can help set the Intention for the Day.

Shape of the Meditation Circle

The Circle is held for about an hour.
We begin by introducing ourselves.

I offer guidance which sets the Intention for the Meditation. This takes the form of an interactive teaching that I present. The teaching is different every time and arises from the specific energies each of you brings to the Circle.

Then, we begin a guided meditation which lasts for 20 minutes.

After the meditation, we all have the opportunity to share what our experience was like. Feel free to share if you wish, or you can remain silent and introspective, as well, if you prefer.

Meditating in a group has a unique energy. It's very different from meditating alone. There is a resonance that accumulates when a community comes together with a like-minded intention.

After we close the Circle, feel free to stay and enjoy casual discussion with light refreshments. This is a good time to reflect on your meditation, share anything you would like with the group, or just socialize!

I have been organizing the Self-Insight Meditation Circle to encourage people who are ready to Transform their lives and Align with their true Path of YourSoul.

It's also a place for people on this same Path to come together and realize that none of us are making this Change alone.

There is a profound Shift occurring, and it's culture-wide. Let's come together and do this work in community!

In changing ourselves, and each other, we change the world. Change starts from within.

Be the Change.

Questions to ask your Essential Self During Meditation

1) What is a problem in my life or a pattern of behavior I wish to change?

2) Why am I behaving in this way? What are the motivations for this behavior? Is this behavior helpful?

3) Rehearse in your mind different possible responses to past or present situations

All of this can happen through Meditation.

The next steps are Action Steps:

1) Practice applying new responses to future situations as they arise

2) Become aware of (notice) ways in which the new patterns are more helpful than past patterns

3) Be compassionate for yourself when occasionally regressing into habitual patterns.

4) Receive & offer compassion from and to others as we all slip back from time to time, but with less frequency.

"Never doubt that a small group of thoughtful, committed citizens can change the world. Indeed, it is the only thing that ever has."
—*Margaret Mead*

Melting Away

Dreams are powerful, and are another gateway ito the meta-conscious mind. Learning to understand what our dreams mean is a very useful skill that can help us align with our Essential Self. They can help us see how our minds are viewing reality and allow us to identify and align (or change) those concepts.

Recently, I had an exceptionally vivid dream that revealed an important insight to me.

I was at a large gathering of family & friends. We had to take a city bus to get to a house that was out in the country where the Milky Way was visible in full regalia.

The gathering was a funeral for an old woman who would die during the course of the dream.

But until the moment of her death, the gathering was more like a birthday party for her. Everyone was there to celebrate and talk and laugh and was sharing all the best things about this woman they could remember.

At the very end of the dream, the old lady followed me into the garage and, having been caressed over the past several hours by everyone sharing all the wonderful things about her, she was completely at Peace with her Life.

She laid down on the concrete floor at my feet, and started to proclaim, "I'm melting! I'm melting!"

And I literally watched her dissolve at my feet.

I said to her, "You are melting. I can see it."

"Really melting?" she asked.

"Really, really melting."

As she dissolved, watching the process was at once extremely terrifying and beautiful. I saw that she had the face of a witch, which made me shudder momentarily.

But that feeling was very brief and, seconds later, there was nothing left of her but her brown robes.

She had transformed from the Wicked Witch into Obi-Wan Kenobi, and a sense of complete peace and calm overcame me.

The old lady is a metaphor for all the old, stale energy in this world that's ready to move on. The way to dissolve that energy is to celebrate all the wonderful good it has done in our lives, and acknowledge how it has served us. We must celebrate it, not kick it to the curb.

We must let it go out of its own free will.

For lack of a better term, we should even "play to its ego."

And then, in that space, when it feels celebrated and acknowledged, it becomes ready to move on, and quite literally melts away.

> *"If you strike me down, I shall become more powerful that you can possibly imagine."*
> —*Obi-Wan Kenobi*

When the old energy melts away, it creates space for the new.

Sometimes, things just need to Realize when they are ready to Transcend, to melt away, to Evolve into something other.

For someone who doesn't really have a spiritual side, it can be quite difficult to accept that the end of this life is near. Because there's no conception that something Different is beyond the horizon.

For others with a profoundly deep Spiritual Intuition, we know that when the Old Fades Away (not just life, but all energies) then on the other side of that transition is something profoundly more beautiful than we can possibly imagine.

> *"Morning has broken, like the first morning.*
> *Blackbird has spoken, like the first bird.*
>
> *Praise for the singing, praise for the morning.*
> *Praise for the springing, fresh from the world.*
>
> *Mine is the sunlight, mine is the morning*
> *Born of the one light Eden saw play."*
>
> —*Cat Stevens,*
> *Morning Has Broken*

Critical Mass

Our world, as it is now, is consumed by toxic, negative energy. It's our mindset. As a culture, we're not happy.

Although there are individuals who prove the exception to this rule, Mother Culture herself has a personality, and that personality currently is very anxious, depressed, and fueled by worry and consumed with negative thoughts.

And it makes sense that Mother Culture should be feeling this way. She's coming up on the very moment when change needs to happen and, like us all on an individual level, she's not yet sure if she's going to be able to do it.

She's terrified that when the moment comes, it's going to pass her by.

That's why I was so anxious for years and years.

That's why so many of us are.

We know we aren't living the life of our dreams, and we're worried we don't have the courage to begin.

Mother Culture knows she needs to change, and she isn't confident it's going to happen.

It will.

There are so many individuals waking up right now, and over the past 3-5 years. We're reaching Critical Mass, approaching the 100th Monkey.

Have you heard the Parable of the 100th Monkey?

I've heard several different versions of it that it's become hard to know which is the original version.

The jist of it is simple.

I'll tell it like a Parable, which I think is a very effective technique for this story.

For readers interested in the true, factual account, please see this Wikipedia page: https://en.wikipedia.org/wiki/Hundredth_monkey_effect

The 100th Monkey Effect

Monkeys were living in isolation on an island that was subject to radioactive fallout from the two nuclear bombs dropped on Japan.

The staple food source of the monkeys was Sweet Potatoes. But all of the nuclear fallout in the soil now made the potatoes toxic, and eating them was killing the monkeys.

One day, one super-intelligent monkey realized what none of the others had: that by washing the potatoes in the ocean, the salt water was able to purify the tubers and make them safe to eat again.

The intelligent monkey showed one of his friends, who

started washing his fruit.

That friend showed his friend, and so on.

But here's the really interesting thing: at first the knowledge catches on slowly, one monkey showing another.

But at some point, once critical mass is reached, then the knowledge spreads .... instantly.

The first, say, 70 monkeys had to show each other how to wash their fruits.

But then, the remaining monkeys started learning the skill without being shown how. They Intuited the knowledge, and it spread instantly.

Then a group of monkeys living in isolation on the other side of the island started doing the same. All at the same time. Not one-by-one, not after having been shown, but simply, instantly, all picked up the fruit-washing behavior.

Fascinating!

The same phenomenon has been observed in carrier pigeons in England after World War II. Pigeons started learning how to open bottles of milk delivered to the front stoops of every home as a government aid plan during a food shortage after the war.

The pigeons, also hungry, and having ample opportunity to practice on thousands of milk bottles left outside, taught themselves how to open the bottles. The knowledge spread one-by-one at first, and then, the rest picked up the new skill seemingly instantaneously after critical mass has been reached.

Then, pigeons on the other side of the world, in Australia, Intuited this exact same skill at the exact same time, having no contact whatsoever with pigeons in England.

This is the instantaneous spread of knowledge once critical mass has been achieved.

So what is critical mass?

The term has its origins in the nuclear age. Critical mass is the amount of material needed to sustain nuclear fission.

But it has more widely caught on the term to explain the 100th Monkey Effect.

From Wikipedia:

"The hundredth monkey effect is a studied phenomenon in which a new behavior or idea is claimed to spread rapidly by unexplained means from one group to all related groups once a critical number of members of one group exhibit the new behavior or acknowledge the new idea."

A New Hope

A New Spirituality, rooted in the fundamental truth that Consciousness Creates Reality, is sweeping across our culture right now.

It's amazing to watch. It's like seeing the sunrise for the first time.

We're washing away, purifying, is a negative, toxic mindset that has been with us for far too long now.

Mother Culture is anxious that we're not going to spread the knowledge and achieve critical mass.

But I see so many of us already waking up, that I believe critical mass is inevitable.

We know now what has to be washed away:

A toxic mindset of greed and negativity.

And we're not just saying no to it, we're replacing it with a new world view:

We have the Secret, the Power of Intention, the Force,

to guide us.

How strong is the Force with you?

To strengthen the Force, go within, meditate.

Identify and catch yourself thinking every time you have a negative thought.

Negative thoughts are the toxic glue that binds our culture together.

Positive thoughts will dissolve the negative ones, like Witches in Rain.

Imagine a completely dark room. Totally black.

One little pinprick of light will shine like a supernova against the complete and total darkness.

In a world of negative thinking, every single positive thought will shine like that same ray of hope in the darkness.

Seek to identify every negative thought you have and turn it into something positive.

Look for the good in people, in every situation.

Use the Force of Conscious Intention and Self-Insight Meditation to reverse negative thought patterns and embrace the light.

For example, if you make a new friend on Facebook, scroll through all the ridiculous posts until you find One that really hits home with you.

Leave a comment about that one that says how wonderful reading it made you feel.

We are all Light Workers weaving a web of Light.

Vibrate the web!

Vibrate the web and we can achieve Critical Mass.

The Power of Positivity

Compliment people! Find something attractive in them, and draw attention to it. At first people might think this is awkward, but do it anyway! We need much more positive reinforcement in our culture.

Ignore the negative.

Focus on the Positive.

This has the power to change someone's day (indeed their entire life) completely.

In improv comedy classes, one technique that's taught and is very effective for insuring the scene continues is: *"Yes, And!"*

So if your fellow actor says something ridiculously absurd like, "I am a sea turtle flying in the air!" you might reply, "Yes! And you're breathing air like water! And I am a bird swimming in the sea!"

That's the Yes, And principle.

Always look for the place of connection to continue the Scene.

Replying to the statement, "I am a sea turtle flying in the air!" with the words, "That's just ridiculous! That's impossible!" simply kills the momentum.

Live your life from the standpoint of Yes, And!

Be positive.

Go out and vibrate the web for everyone, and keep it vibrating with positive energy. Everyone you reach will then vibrate the web in a positive way.

Pay it forward.

If someone compliments you, return the compliment

with something positive in response: meet a compliment with another compliment, instead of your knee-jerk reaction of feeling awkward and bashful.

Pay it forward.

Pass it on.

Vibrate the web.

Because the person you reach will then go out and vibrate the web for the next person.

One-by-one until critical mass is achieved and the new worldview begins to spontaneously catch on for everyone. We are constantly affecting everyone we interact with, all the time, in subtle and profound ways we can't possibly imagine.

I saw someone crossing the street the other day and she had a very interesting look about her.

I smiled and told her so.

"Interesting style! I like it!" I told her with a smile.

As we crossed the street in opposite directions, I heard her giggle happily and continue walking on.

My comment gave her cause to have a little bit more happiness that day. Wherever she was going, she probably arrived with a smile.

And someone else saw it, and it made their day, and so on. One-by-one we change the world.

Everything is interconnected.

Standing in line at a grocery store, the person ahead of you often looks agitated, impatient.

Notice that person's bracelet or necklace, or tie-dye tee-shirt, something, anything, unique about them that you resonate positively with.

Don't notice their agitated demeanor.

Re-train your brain to see the positive and tune-out the negative.

Don't engage with the negative.

If you notice a beautiful tie-dye t-shirt, ask the person wearing it, "Wow! Cool shirt. Did you make that yourself?"

One compliment can be a pinprick of light and transform a person's negative day from the outside-in.

One-by-one we change the world.

Everything is interconnected.

Indra's Web

The Mutual Interdependence of all things is one of the core beliefs of Buddhism that really resonates with me.

We are all deeply interconnected, and all affect each other in more profound ways that we can possibly imagine.

Buddhists have a beautiful vision of the Universe:

Imagine a Spiderweb at dawn, each thread of the web glistening with morning dew.

Each dew is glinting with the morning sun, newly rising.

And within each dew drop is contained the reflection of every other dew drop, and every other reflection of the sun reflected in every other dewdrop.

And you are just a dew-drop, reflecting the sun and every other dew drop around you.

Each of us reflects every other dew drop surrounding us.

The entire web is reflected in every little part.

When an insect lands somewhere on the web, every

fiber of the web vibrates.

This image is known as Indra's Web, and illustrates the mutual interdependence of all things.

And we are the weavers of the web.

As we act, so do we vibrate the web and everything contained within it.

Western Science shows us this is true as well.

Contained in every single strand of DNA, is all the information necessary to clone a whole person.

Art and poetry have also presented to the same notion, as in the opening lines of William Blake's poem, Auguries of Innocence and Arthur O'Shaughnessy's Ode.

> "To see a World in a Grain of Sand
> And a Heaven in a Wild Flower
> Hold Infinity in the palm of your hand
> And Eternity in an hour."
> —William Blake

> "We are the music makers,
> And we are the dreamers of dreams."
> —Arthur O'Shaughnessy

Mirror Work

In every dew drop, in every grain of sand, is reflected all of Infinity. And it's the infinity we create, and it starts in our own minds.

If our own mindsets are toxic, we will vibrate the web in that way.

If our own mindsets are positive, the web vibrates like beautiful music.

We have discussed the idea of Self-Insight Meditation as one key way to identify you're really thinking, and how to change that mindset upon realizing the ways it no longer serves us.

But change can be very hard. And frightening.

And true connection with another person can be terrifying at first.

But when we approach each other from a place of connection, instead of disconnection, and train our minds to always look for the place of connection, then we truly make a difference.

Getting started is always the hardest part.

Sitting along in silence, with your own thoughts, can be terribly frightening.

> *"Staring our inner demons in the face is so uncomfortable that it can make crawling through broken glass dipped in alcohol and rattlesnake venom seem like a cakewalk. It is a rare person who's willing to do this without being prodded into it."*
> —*Franklin Veaux & Eve Rickert,*
> *"More than Two"*

Are you willing to try?

If so, here's a technique you can practice at home. It's super-easy to do! It's also the hardest thing you'll ever do ... and the most rewardning.

Think that meditating in a dark room with your eyes closed sounds scary? Try this!

Find a mirror. Sit down in front of it, and stare at yourself. Don't look away.

Look yourself in the eyes.

See what's going on in there.

Do you like what you see?

No?

So change it.

Tell yourself, "I love you, you're perfect, now change for the better!"

The relationship with yourself is the single most important relationship you will ever have in your life.

> *"It's by far the hardest thing I've ever done.*
> *To be so in love with you and so alone."*
> *—Peter, Paul & Mary*

> *"A person who loves themselves*
> *will never be alone."*
> *—Unknown*

And here's my favorite love song that I've ever heard. But instead of thinking of the pronouns "I" and "you" as being separate people, imagine them both being the same person: You!

> *"How my feet want to jump up.*
> *Take me high to the sky.*
> *I found you.*
> *How my heart is beaming like the sun*
> *and the moon and the starts beyond.*
> *I found you...I found you...I found you."*
> *—Luluc*

Waves Crashing on the Shore

Imagine this mindset:
You are sitting on the shore of a beautiful island. Beautiful palm trees at your back, sea gulls chirping overhead. It's a beautiful place.

This is where you live now, your current life. It has its problems, but in general, you have mostly everything you need, and you're comfortable here.

You're sitting on the beach, overlooking the ocean before you, watching the waves come in.

And in the distance, you see another island.

And gazing at this island, although you can't see it clearly from here, you know that's the Life of Your Dreams.

We have to spend time imagining what this island looks like in order to create it. Consciousness creates reality, afterall. Nevertheless, you can't conceptualize every tree, animal or all of the beautiful cliffs and vantage points on that Island until you actually get there.

We need to conceptualize the Life of Our Dreams, but leave the details to the Higher Consciousness of creation. Have faith that the island of your dreams you have conceived of in your mind is going to be far more beautiful than anything you can possibly conceive of staring at it from this distant shore.

So, you've spent the time, done the personal work necessary to conceptualize what the Life of your Dreams looks like; that's what manifested the island.

You've been sitting here on this distant shore staring at it for some time now. The vision is clear enough, but not crystal, and that's okay. That's where faith comes in.

You've been sitting on this shore for weeks now, maybe months or years, thinking about swimming over there, but consumed by fear of the unknown.

But like Tom Hanks in *Cast Away*, there simply comes a time when you Know you need to Go. That moment doesn't come simply when you think you're ready, but when Spirit compels you to go.

It's not good enough to simply feel like you can't sit still any longer. You need to feel the pull to Go!

When you feel the pull, the urge, to just take the plunge and dive in, that's Spirit, compelling you.

And don't start swimming until Spirit compels you. And when Spirit does compels you, it will feel like a golden thread extending from heaven into your heart center, with some higher power tugging on the other end.

It won't feel like you're just ready to go, but that you

have to go. That you *must* go.

And you're going to have to swim.

You may feel a profound sense of depression and anxiety accumulating up to the moment you take the great leap of faith and plunge headlong into the ocean.

Anxiety is the feeling that arises when the way you are currently vibrating in your life is creating an interference pattern with the way your Soul knows it needs to vibrate. It is those two vibrations interfering with each other, and you standing right in the middle, that manifests as an overwhelming sense of anxiety.

This might go on for months or years.

The good news is you can decide to use that energy that's manifesting as anxiety for a higher purpose.

The cure for anxiety and depression is neither pills nor drugs, it's simply letting go of everything that is not aligned with your the True Path of YourSoul.

At the very moment of letting go, the anxiety and depression evaporate and you feel, for once, truly free, and you then you plunge into the water, and resolve to to swim to a new shore.

You're not in the clear quite yet, though. You've made the decision to go. That was the relatively easy part compared to what comes next.

Now you have swim and fight against all the breaker waves crashing onto the shore you're leaving behind.

If you started swimming before Spirit compelled you, the breaker waves are going to be too powerful for you to overcome. They will turn you back to shore, or destroy your boat, or force you back to the island you came from.

But when you swim with Spirit out into the waves, despite their sheer power, you will have the guidance, perseverance and dedication necessary to push through them.

The connection to the Golden Thread in your heart center won't break. It will keep you from drowning.

There might be five breaker waves or ten or twenty! That depends how much you have to fight through, and it's different for each person.

The Breaker Waves are all the various components of your current life you're leaving behind.

But trust that once you get through the last breaker wave, it's calm, open ocean.

It will be a pleasant swim, as soon as the breaker waves are met with perseverance and resolve and broken through.

Now you're swimming in the open ocean towards the other island, and it's getting closer, and closer, and closer.

Soon, the water begins creating new waves, but this time they're pulling you toward the new shoreline.

Now the waves are working with you, not against you.

At this point, you have gone from actively Pursuing your Dreams to your Dreams Pursuing You.

The waves are pulling you ever closer and closer to the Island of your Dreams.

And then, in the very next moment, you feel the soft sand squish between your toes, and you begin to crawl like a newborn onto the shore.

And now you fall to your knees, tears streaming down

your face, in the sure and certain knowledge that you have arrived on the shores of the Life of your Dreams.

Rejoice! You have all of your life ahead of you now to explore, frolic, and greet the new life you have worked so hard at achieving.

And it's more beautiful than anything you have ever imagined.

> *"Make the most of yourself,*
> *for that is all there is of you."*
> —*Ralph Waldo Emerson*

Afterword

Personal Maxims of a Positive Enabler

The following three sets of three maxims are my personal compass for how I align my mindset with my intentions, actions and interactions to the best of my ability.

I didn't develop this list and then start living according to it. Rather, this list emerged organically as I was observing the transformation of my own life over a period of several years.

One day I woke up and realized, "Wow, self, you're actually happy, consistently and really. What the heck have we started doing right that's allowed us to be actually, really, fundamentally, be happy?"

To the best of my ability, here is the answer to that question:

Mindset Maxims

1. Always work towards Revealing Truth.
To you yourself and others.
Realize that blunt honesty can do as much harm as lying.
So reveal truth gently, and never conceal it.

2. Cultivate positive, personal experience.
Look for the positive and engage with it.
Don't ignore the negative.
Identify the negative, but don't feed it.

3. Reveal the joy & absurdity in all things
Even when it's a pain in the ass, don't focus on the pain.
Rather, laugh at the absurd shape of the paddle.

Personal Growth

1. Identify, question, then embrace or transcend your personal patterns.
First, realize why you're doing what you're doing.
Is it working? Great! Embrace it!
Does it suck? Fuck! So change it.

2. See the symbolic nature of all things
Everything we see reveals how our mind is interpreting the world around us. Everything is evidence of who we are.

3. Know & Accept Thyself
Never run from who you are.
Turn and look at yourself in the mirror.
Smile and wave! (But don't be creepy about it.)

Nurturing Relationships

1. Transcend expectations!
Expectations suffocate relationships.

2. Allow the ego to serve the soul
When you want something, approach desire from a mindset of, "I want this only if it's best for everyone."

3. Prioritize quality time
Ideally in the morning, because what you do first thing sets the tone for the rest of the day.

Number 4 for All:

4. Don't push too hard, but keep making progress.
Whether you're a tortoise or a hair, go at your own pace. It's actually not a race, but a journey.
When you're looking for your pot of gold, remember to look up and appreciate the rainbow guiding you there.

These Maxims, especially the ones under Nurturing Relationships, are guidelines, but need much more elaboration. It is my intention for them to be the foundation next book.

About the Author

Tom Tortorich is an author, motivational speaker and Buddhist-y life coach.

He is a student of *Bön: the Tibetan Art of Positive Thinking* and has been called a "Positive Enabler" by many people who he has inspired to begin pursuing the life of their dreams.

In 2014, he quit his day job as a highly paid web designer to follow his dreams.

Don't Read this Book! is Tom's fourth book.

His other works include a novel titled *Time Without End*, and two collections of essays titled, *A People's History of Capitalism* and *The Evolution of Thought*.

Tom currently lives in Kansas City, Missouri where he leads meditation classes, workshops, and motivational speaking events. Support Tom's goal to offer a Ted Talk within the next 3-5 years titled, "Don't Meditate! It may cause a mid-life crisis!"

*Visit Tom online at **www.PositiveEnabler.com** where you can find links to:*
- *Join the Positive Enabler Facebook Community*
- *Find out about upcoming meditation classes & events*
- *Watch Tom's "Daily Tao" videos on YouTube*

www.ingramcontent.com/pod-product-compliance
Lightning Source LLC
Chambersburg PA
CBHW071218090426
42736CB00014B/2885